Pictish Warrior
AD 297–841

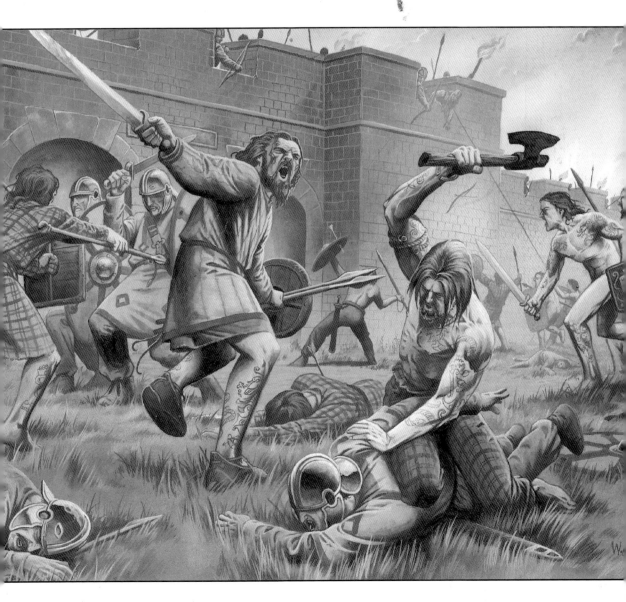

Paul Wagner • Illustrated by Wayne Reynolds

First published in Great Britain in 2002 by Osprey Publishing,
Midland House, West Way, Botley, Oxford OX2 0PH, UK
443 Park Avenue South, New York, NY 10016, USA
Email: info@ospreypublishing.com

CIP Data for this publication is available from the British Library

ISBN 1 84176 346 2

Editor: Nikolai Bogdanovic
Editorial consultant: Angus Konstam
Design: Ken Vail Graphic Design, Cambridge, UK
Index by Alison Worthington
Originated by Magnet Harlequin, Uxbridge, UK
Printed in China through World Print Ltd.

05 06 07 10 9 8 7 6 5 4 3

FOR A CATALOGUE OF ALL BOOKS PUBLISHED
BY OSPREY PLEASE CONTACT:

NORTH AMERICA
Osprey Direct, 2427 Bond Street,
University Park, IL 60466, USA
E-mail: info@ospreydirectusa.com

ALL OTHER REGIONS
Osprey Direct UK, P.O. Box 140, Wellingborough,
Northants, NN8 2FA, UK
E-mail: info@ospreydirect.co.uk

www.ospreypublishing.com

Artist's note

Readers may care to note that the original paintings from
which the colour plates in this book were prepared are
available for private sale. All reproduction copyright
whatsoever is retained by the Publishers. All enquiries
should be addressed to:

Wayne Reynolds
20 Woodside Place
Burley, Leeds LS4 2QU, UK

The Publishers regret that they can enter into no
correspondence upon this matter.

Dedication

To my daughter Veronica, Warrior Princess

Acknowledgements

My sincere thanks to all who have helped in the preparation
of this book, especially the very knowledgeable members
of the Celtic Martial Arts Research Society, and to my wife
Julie, for her patience and support.
All illustrations are the author's own unless otherwise
indicated.

CONTENTS

PICTISH WARRIOR AD 297–841

INTRODUCTION

The Picts have captured the public imagination in a manner unlike any other ancient people. Exotic and mysterious, their name conjures up images of sun-worshipping naked warriors, covered in blue body paint, storming down from the icy north to tear the Roman legionaries down from Hadrian's Wall. They emerged from a murky past to dominate northern Britain for over 500 years, and then vanished just as mysteriously, becoming mere legend and leaving their successors to puzzle and argue over their curious artefacts.

While there are elements of truth in this picture, the Picts hold an important place in the history of Britain for more prosaic reasons. They represent a high point of Celtic civilisation, remaining free and unconquered beyond the borders of the Roman world, and rising to become the first barbarians to form a recognisable 'nation'.

There is no denying that the aura of mystery that surrounds the Picts is well deserved. They are first mentioned by name in AD 297, though it is clear from the context that they had been a problem for the Romano-British for some time. But for how long? Why were they not mentioned before? Were the Picts indigenous to northern Britain, or Celtic incomers? Was 'Pict' their native name, or a Roman nickname? Was their language Celtic? If so, was it related to British or Gaelic? Did they really adopt matrilinear succession? Did they paint their bodies? What were the meanings of Pictish symbols? Why were the 'symbol stones' set up? Were they pagan or Christian? And how and why did the Picts disappear?

Who were the Picts?

The word 'pict' is usually said to derive from the Latin *pictus*, meaning 'painted', in reference to the Picts' habit of tattooing their bodies. While there seems no reason to doubt that the Picts followed this practice, as an explanation of the word it is somewhat inadequate. There seems no need for the Romans to invent a new name for a tattooed people, for they

A fanciful engraving of a Pict from 1590.

A (slightly) better reconstruction by Robert Havell, 1815.

ere familiar with many such tribes, and none of the Latin descriptions ctually use the word *pictum* to describe Celtic tattoos.

There are several alternative interpretations of the meaning of 'pict'. he 4th-century military historian Vegetius recorded that the British ord *pictas* referred to a camouflaged scout boat, coloured sea-blue r *pictae*. In Welsh, this boat was a *peithas*, the sailors were *peithi*, and he Picts were *peithwyr*, while medieval Irish chronicles called it *picard*, and interchange the name *Picti* or *Pictones* with *piccardach* or *icars* ('pirates').

The way the Romans used the word, however, was as a tribal ame, such as 'savage tribes of *Scotti* and *Picti*'. Pict in Old Norse is *Pettr*', Old English '*Poehta*' and Old Scots '*Pecht*', all of which seem o be variations on a real name, not a slang term for either painted' or 'pirate'. It thus seems likely that *Picti* was a proper ame, and the punning reference to bodily decoration was nerely a happy coincidence.

But who were the Picts? The simplest answer is 'the inhabitants f northern Britain from AD 297–858', which might be factually ccurate but is otherwise unenlightening. It does, however, draw ttention to the first puzzling thing about the Picts; that they are bsent, at least by name, from the first two centuries of Roman nteraction with northern Britain.

In the first centuries AD the land north of the Forth was eopled by two broad cultural groups. In the central lighlands was a tribal confederacy of Britons, most notably ne *Caledonii*, whose ancestry dated back to the 8th century BC, hen timber-laced hill forts, ironworking and the other marks

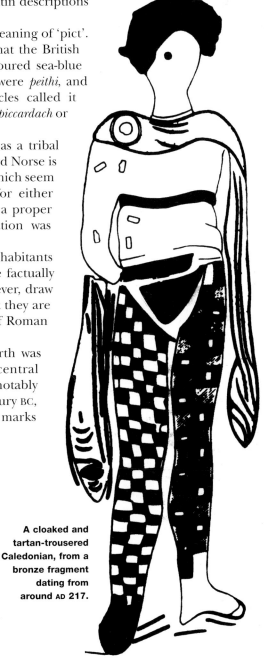

A cloaked and tartan-trousered Caledonian, from a bronze fragment dating from around AD 217.

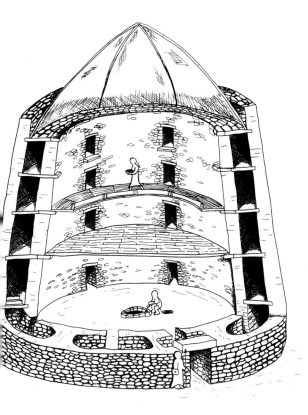

Brochs were a type of circular dry stone fort with an inner courtyard of about 10 metres (32 ft) in diameter, containing a central well. The 3.6 metre-thick (12 ft) walls had internal stairs and chambers, and there may have been wooden floors or balconies on the upper levels and a thatched or hide roof. Brochs are sometimes compared to medieval castles, but perhaps a better parallel would be the similarly sized stronghouses of the 16th century Border Reiver clans.

of Celtic culture first arrived in Scotland. In the Orkneys, Shetland, th Hebrides and the far north-west of Scotland another group built different sort of fort, a type of circular drystone tower called a 'broch of which over 500 were built between the 1st century BC and th 2nd century AD. Although the hill forts have a much longer ancestr than the brochs, both remained in use at the same time, and there wer clear cultural and political divisions between the inhabitants.

Roman dealings with the Orkneys, recorded by Pliny the Elder an Tacitus, indicate that the broch-dwellers petitioned to be allies of Rome The Orkneys made formal submission to Rome in AD 43, and later ser envoys to ask for Roman protection, the direct result of which wa Agricola's invasion of Scotland and the battle of Mons Grampius i AD 84. After the battle, Agricola's fleet went on to receive the forma submission of Orkney. The brochs have yielded a rich diversity of hig status Roman artefacts and local copies of Roman objects, suggestin Roman support and a sophisticated trading network, which could nc have existed without Roman acquiescence.

Following Agricola's withdrawal, the Caledonian tribes fought successful guerrilla war against the Romans, which eventually resulted i the construction of Hadrian's Wall and the Antonine Wall. The followin centuries saw escalating Caledonian raids until, in AD 208, Empero Septimus Severus himself came to Britain to deal with the barbarian: Severus did not try to bring the Caledonians to battle, but aimed to wip them out by systematic devastation of the landscape, hanging the nativ chiefs, burning the crops, killing the livestock, and destroying the hi forts by setting the timber-laced walls on fire, melting or 'vitrifying' th

Pictish predators. The top-left wolf, from 4th-century Orkney, is one of the earliest known Pictish carvings.

6

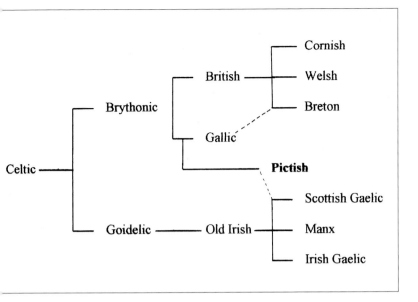

...one. Severus' policy, in other words, was nothing short of 'ethnic cleansing', and it seems to have been extremely successful. There was nearly a century of peace, and when Scotland once more entered history it was ruled by the Picts.

There have been many explanations for this turn of events. Some believe that the Picts were merely the descendants of the Caledonian Britons, or the resurgent remnants of pre-Celtic aboriginals. Others believe they can identify a substratum of Gaelic place names, and conclude the Picts were an earlier Goidelic-speaking Celtic society. Others have seen a connection with the *Pictones* or *Pictes*, a seafaring tribe from the Biscay coast who aided Caesar against the *Veneti* (a Gaulish seafaring tribe from Amorica) and suggest they may have arrived in Britain in a migratory movement comparable to those that brought the *Belgae*, *Scotti* and Anglo-Saxons. Others, accepting mythological tales of Scythian origin, have postulated that the fathers of the Picts were Sarmatians in Roman service, who established a dynasty over the natives.

Some of these theories obviously fit the evidence better than others. For example, Gaelic speakers like St Columba could converse with the Britons of Strathclyde without difficulty, but needed translators to talk to the Picts, and Bede stated quite unequivocally that Pictish was a fourth, separate language alongside British, Gaelic and English. In 1955 Kenneth Jackson determined that Pictish belonged to the Brythonic branch of Celtic languages, with features found in Gaulish but not in British, and suggested a pre-Indoeuropean substratum based on a few indecipherable ogham inscriptions. There has been little advance on this analysis since, except a refutation of the non-Celtic element.

There are also a number of diversions that have confused scholars. For instance, Irish chroniclers refer to both the non-Gaelic inhabitants of early Ireland and the Picts as *Cruithni*. Some have used this to support the argument that the Picts were aboriginals, whereas in fact *Cruithni* is simply the Goidelic rendering of *Pritani* or 'Briton'. This has, in turn, been used to identify the Picts as the Caledonians. Unfortunately, on closer inspection the early Irish authors use the name *Cruithni* only to refer to the Northern Irish, and use *Picti* for the North British. The *Cruithni* of Ireland were defeated in the battle of Brae Slieve in 627 and are not mentioned again after 774, while the name *Cruithni* is not used to refer to the Picts until 865, by which time the Picts had lost their separate identity. The confusion seems to have arisen partly because the *Scotti* were themselves *Cruithni*, and because the legendary 'Father of the Picts' bore the personal name Cruithne.

In fact the earliest identifiable evidence of Pictish culture comes from the broch-dwellers of the north. While the earliest Pictish symbol stones date from the 6th or even 7th century AD, at Pool in Orkney a 6th-century Pictish building was built with re-used stones which already had Pictish symbols on them. A bone pin and a cattle phalanx from Orkney, carbon-dated to the 4th and 5th centuries AD respectively, also had carved Pictish symbols. Outside the broch at Carn Liath, Caithness, a local silver copy of a Roman 'crossbow brooch' was found, adorned with Pictish symbols, and made prior to the 5th century AD.

Written history also favours the brochs as the cradle of the Picts. Like the Vikings, the broch-dwellers found Orkney an ideal staging post for piracy, and during the Pictish raids of the 4th century the Roman fleet targeted the Orkneys and Shetland for reprisals, not the south. Chroniclers like Nennius, Bede and Gildas all indicate that Orkney was the first centre of Pictish power, and the Pictish place-name element *pit* is widely found in the broch-lands, despite the later obliteration of place-names by Norse settlers. The Vikings named Orkney *terra Petorum* ('Pict land') and her channel the *Pettaland fjord* ('Pictland Firth', now Pentland Firth). Oral tradition also links the brochs to the Picts, and they are called 'Picts' houses' in Scotland to this day. After Mons Grampius, brochs even began to appear around the Firth of Forth, marking an expansion south by the broch-dwellers, perhaps under Roman invitation. In the century after the campaign of Severus, archaeology reveals a major political upheaval in the north-east and Highlands, with the emergence of wealthy rulers who could afford sumptuous metalwork and high-status Roman commodities.

If this new elite were the broch-dwellers and future Picts, this still does not answer the question 'who were the Picts?' The broch-dwellers may have been ancient inhabitants, Britons related to the Caledonians, an earlier settlement of Celts, or an incoming settlement of Gaulish refugees, and trying to identify the influence of one group of Celts on another is all but impossible. For example, whether the brochs were commissioned by native warlords or incoming pirates, their construction is bound to (and does) derive largely from a common native building tradition.

It is not unreasonable to presume that the bulk of the Pictish population would have been descendants of the age-old inhabitants of the area, and that the culture of the Caledonians would have made a major contribution to Pictish society, even if there was some kind of cultural-political coup. However, the overall identity of early medieval societies was largely determined by the culture of their warrior elite, so it is probably more important to examine what the Picts themselves believed of their own origins.

The Pictish foundation myth

The *Pictish Chronicle* is a collection of medieval manuscripts containing several lists of Pictish kings, counting from a century or two BC to the mid-9th century AD. The 'Pictish foundation myth' that precedes the king-lists tells how Cruithne, the father of the Picts, arrived from Scythia and reigned for 100 years. He divided the land into seven areas, named after each of his seven sons:

'Seven sons of Cruithne then
Into seven divided Alban,
Cait, Ce, Cirig, a warlike clan
Fib, Fidach, Fotla, Fortrenn'.

These seven kingdoms are readily identified: *Fib* is Fife, *Cait* is Caithness, *Fotlaig* is Atfodla (Atholl), and *Fortrenn* was the district around Mentieth and Strathearn. *Cirig* can be traced to *Maghcircin*, the 'Plains of Circinn', now Mearns. *Ce* survives in Bennachie in Aberdeenshire, leaving *Fidach* as the area around the Moray Firth. These areas match closely those historically occupied by the Picts, who were not found in Argyll, nor along the western coast south of Skye, the closest Pictish colony to Iona.

A portrait of a Pict from Shetland.

It has been suggested that the Pictish foundation myth was political propaganda, designed to unite the warring tribes into a single nation, or to legitimise a ruling dynasty, or perhaps to confirm Scottish sovereignty in Argyll. Celtic oral tradition, however, is a source to be respected, and even such obvious mythology as this should not be dismissed unhesitatingly, especially when other sources tell essentially the same tale. Gildas, a 6th-century British monk, brings the Picts hairy and unclothed in *currachs* (small hide boats) from the north across the sea, and states that not until the final departure of the Romans did the Picts settle down in Scotland 'for the first time', as they 'seized the whole northern part of the land as far as the wall, to the exclusion of the inhabitants', clearly indicating that the Picts were not considered natives. Nennius, another British monk who, around AD 800, compiled a history from all the older documents he could find, also says that they settled first in Orkney and then moved south to conquer a third of Britain. According to Bede, the mostly reliable Northumbrian cleric writing in the late 7th and early 8th century, the Picts arrived in a few boats, driven around Britain by a storm. They eventually landed in northern Ireland and asked permission to settle, but were told there was no land to spare, and they should try northern Britain.

So the Picts crossed into Britain and began to settle in the north of the island, since the Britons were in possession of the south. Having no women with them, these Picts asked wives of the Irish, who consented on condition that, when any dispute arose, they should choose a king from the female royal line rather than the male. This custom continues among the Picts to this day.

Some believe that this story was invented to legitimise the Scottish takeover of the Pictish throne. This is unlikely, as when Bede was writing the disorganised Scots had just been conquered by the Picts. It is also worth remembering that the first Norse pirates who arrived in Orkney Man and the Western Isles did so without women, and had to take them from the native population, while the remnants of Magnus Maximus army who settled in Brittany in the late 4th century also arrived without women, and so killed the American men and cut out the women's tongues 'lest the pure British speech be corrupted', so the Pictish tale is not without precedent. There is also reason to believe that the Pictish acquisition of women may not have been entirely peaceful; an ancient Irish poem *Duan Gircanash* records how 300 Irish women were kidnapped by the womenless Picts.

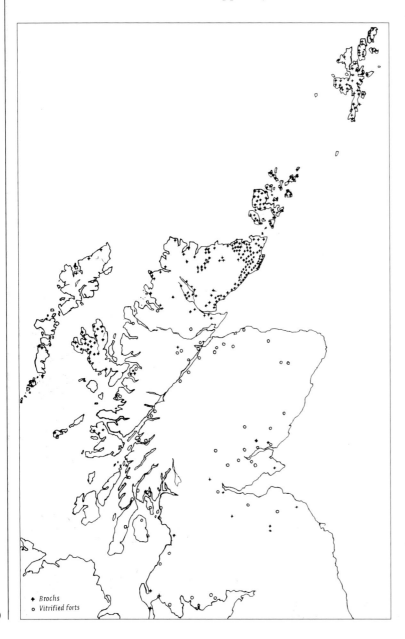

The distribution of brochs and vitrified hill forts.

- ✦ *Brochs*
- ○ *Vitrified forts*

'Cruithne, son of Cuig,
took their women from
them
It is directly stated
Except Tea, wife of
Hermion
Son of Miledh…

There were no charming,
noble wives
For their young men;
Their women having
been stolen…'

Other Welsh and Irish versions of the story add more detail, but the basic thrust was that the Picts originated as warriors who came from across the seas and first settled in the far north of the country. They had to obtain Irish women, for which Cruithne 'swore by the heaven and the earth, the sun and the moon, the sea and the land, the dew and the elements, that on women should be the Royal succession among them for ever', and they were implacable enemies of the native Britons whom they eventually conquered. Whatever the truth in the story, it was an important core belief. As a commonly held myth it gave the Picts a sense of 'national identity', and helped to weld them into a powerful and united political entity.

CHRONOLOGY

AD

297	The Picts are first mentioned by name as raiding northern Britain.
305	Constantius restores Hadrian's Wall and campaigns against 'Caledonians and other Picts' before dying in 306.
343	Rome enters into a truce with the Picts.
360-67	Ammianus Marcellinus writes that 'The Picti, Saxones, Scotti and Atecotti harassed the Britons continually'.
368	The Barbarian Conspiracy. A massive attack is launched by the Picts, Scots and Saxons on Roman Britain. Theodosius pursues the raiding parties by land and sea, and campaigns 'beyond the Wall'.
382-83	Pictish raid on Britain.
396	Scots and Picts raid Britain. Stilicho drives them out.
c.423	St Germanus visits Britain and takes part in the 'Hallelujah victory' over a joint Pictish and Saxon raid.
449	Vortigern hires Saxon mercenaries to stop Pictish raiding, who attack Orkney and campaign 'as far as the borders of the Picts'.
c.450	St Ninian begins conversion of the Southern Picts.
c.455	Picts attack Roman Britain in support of the Saxon rebellion.
455-60	Coel Hen of the Britons raids Scots and Picts, setting them against each other.
c.460	The king of Irish Dalriata, Fergus mor Mac Erc, arrives in Argyll and forms an alliance with the Picts. Together they defeat and kill Coel Hen at Coilsfield.
c.500	Fresh immigration of Scotti from northern Ireland.
c.508-14	Most likely period of the Arthurian era. The Picts are expelled from the Lowlands.
537	King of Scots, Comgall mac Fergus, killed by Picts.
558	King of Scots, Gabran mac Fergus, killed by Picts.
561-70	St Columba arrives in Scotland, begins missionary work and visits the Northern Pictish King Bridei in Inverness.
580	Aeden MacGabrain of Dalriada campaigns against the Picts of Orkney.
600	Isidore of Seville writes about Pictish tattoos.
c.630	Domnall Brecc leads an army against the Irish High King, but is defeated at the battle of Moira. Last dynastic link between the Dalriadan Scots and Ireland is severed.
c.660	Oswiu of Northumbria claims overlordship of Picts.
664	Synod of Whitby. Roman church takes precedence over Celtic church.
670	Oswiu dies.
672	Ecgfrith, son of Oswiu, attacks and destroys a Pictish army at the battle of Carron.
674	Ecgfrith withdraws from Alba to fight the Mercians.
681	Picts take Dunnottar back from the Northumbrians.
682	Picts retake Orkney from the Scots.
683	Picts lay waste to Scottish capital Dunnadd.
685	Picts destroy the Northumbrian army at the battle of Dunnichen.
698	A Northumbrian army invades the lands of the Picts and is destroyed. Adomnan of Iona makes the 'law of the innocents' excluding women from military service.
711	The Northumbrians rout the Pictish army on Plain of Manaw between the rivers Avon and Carron.
713	Picts and Northumbrians make peace.
717	Nechtan, King of Picts, brings the Pictish church into line with Rome and expels Columban monks 'across the spine of Britain'.
724-29	Southern Pictish civil war over the crown. Oengus emerges victorious.
730	Oengus captures and drowns the 'King of Atholl', gaining overlordship of both the Northern and Southern Picts.
736	Oengus invades Dalriada, beheads the Scottish king, and proclaims himself the first King of Picts and Scots.
738	A war fleet of 150 Pictish ships is wrecked by storm near Ross.
741	A 'devastating attack' is executed on the Scots by Picts.

Pictish serpent imagery. The meaning of such symbols is lost.

11

744	Oengus attacks and defeats the Britons of Strathclyde.
750	Oengus' brother Talorcan is defeated by the Britons of Strathclyde at the battle of Mocetwawc.
756	Oengus makes an alliance with Eadbeorht of Northumbria and attacks Dumbarton. The Britons break the siege and seize Eadbeorht's northern lands.
761	Oengus dies, and the Scots break free from Pictish rule.
768	King of Scots, Aed Finn, invades Alba and fights the Pictish king Ciniod in Fortriu (Fortrenn).
782	Causantin Mac Fergus of Dalriada kills Dubhtollarg, king of the Southern Picts.
789	Causantin Mac Fergus defeats Northern Picts and becomes the first Scottish king of both Scots and Picts.
c.780-90	Norwegian settlers arrive in Orkney and overwhelm the local Picts. Orkney becomes the staging point for Viking raids.
820	Causantin Mac Fergus dies, and Picts re-establish their dynasty over the Scots.
825	Viking raids force the evacuation of Iona.
834	Scottish leader Alpin rebels during a Viking raid, defeats one Pictish army, but is killed by a second Pictish force.
839	Pictish King and 'numberless others' are killed in battle with the Vikings. Alpin's son Kenneth makes a claim for the throne, but is passed over in favour of Drust IX.
841	Kenneth MacAlpine becomes Rex Pictorum.
858	Domnall I unites Picts and Scots under a Scottish ruling dynasty.

Romans riding down naked, barbaric northerners. From the Bridgeness slab of the Antonine Wall.

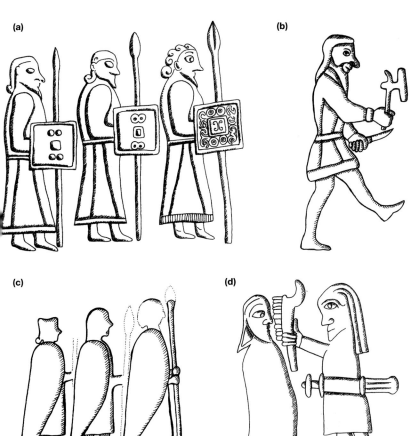

(a)

(b)

(c)

(d)

Pictish warriors
(a) The *Three Kings* from Orkney.
(b) This figure from Golspie, Sutherland, is armed with an axe and knife.
(c) Three spear-armed men from Eassie. The 'wings' are probably cloaks.
(d) *Sampson* wearing a sword and holding the jawbone of an ass, from Inchbrayock.

PICTISH HEROIC SOCIETY

The Picts left no written descriptions of their lives, history, myths or society. While their physical remains and remarkable carvings can provide some detail, it is a simple fact that little meaningful can be said about the life of the Pictish warrior without drawing extensively from evidence from other Celtic peoples. Fortunately, the remarkable uniformity and conservatism of Celtic culture makes this a reasonable thing to do. In particular, the Irish epics, those 'windows to the Dark Ages', have important insights because the Irish heroes actually visit Alba on numerous occasions. Many Highland clans also claim descent from Pictish ancestors, and the very close parallels between medieval Welsh and Highland social structure suggests that Highland clans owed a great deal more to Brythonic/Pictish roots than to Irish; certainly more than has generally been considered.

Despite the aura of mystery around them, the Picts did not exist in isolation. From the first we hear of them, the Picts were in close contact with the Irish, Scots, Britons and Anglo-Saxons, and probably adhered to a typical dark-age British culture. Much of what can be reconstructed of the Pictish warrior's life would apply equally to a Briton or an Irish warrior. However, there are also some discernible points of difference.

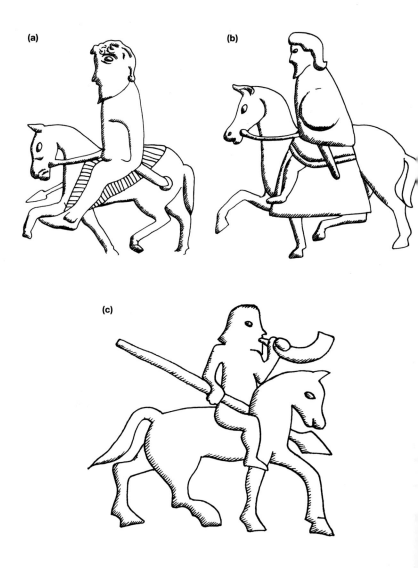

Two different breeds of horse can be discerned on Pictish stones. The most common (a & b) is the small native pony or Highland *garron*, surviving as the Eriskay pony. The larger animal (c) is probably related to the Fell pony, and to the extinct 'Galloway' heavy horse.

Pictish society was essentially tribal or clan-based, but they appear to have been politically more centralised than their neighbours. Their nation was divided into seven kingdoms, each with its own 'king', later known as the *toiseach*, *mormaer* or 'great steward', who wielded judicial power and led the provincial armies in war. Each king also had a *tannis* or designated heir who acted as a deputy ruler, and there were sub-kings who ruled over independent regions; the ruler of Orkney, for example, was described as a *subregulus*.

Above these regional kings were the High Kings, one for the 'Northern Picts' and another of the 'Southern Picts'. The Southern Picts were spread over Atholl, Circinn, Fife and Fortrenn, while the Northern Picts occupied Caithness, Moray and Aberdeenshire. The relationship between them is unclear, but it was perhaps analogous to the Northern and Southern Ui Neill in Ireland, the Southern Picts being the senior branch. The division makes geographic sense, with the Mounth presenting a formidable physical barrier, and for some time the Southern Picts were Christian and the Northern Picts still pagan.

However, the Pictish king-lists show the situation was really more complicated, with periods where there was only a single High King ruling both, while some High Kings reigned more than once, alone or in partnership with others.

Below the kings were the tribal chieftains and their extended families. Genealogy was important to all Celtic societies, whether the Gaelic *cinel* or *clann* or the Welsh *cenedl*, and the Picts were no different. The clan was made up of sub-clans or *septs*, bound together by perceived descent from a common ancestor, and groups of related clans made up the tribe or kingdom. Unlike the fragmented Highland society of the 16th–18th centuries, however, Pictish clans were not self-governing, militarily independent units. Their importance was primarily social and legal, as the kinship group was responsible for the actions of its members, and even in 12th-century Scottish law, the *cenedl* was responsible for paying the *wergild* or *galnys*, a fine assessed in cattle, to the family of a murder victim.

At the top of the clan hierarchy were what the Welsh called the *uchelwyr* ('higher men'), or the *daoine uaisle* of the Highland clans. It was from this class that the bulk of the Pictish warriors would have been drawn; Strabo noted that the warrior bands of the Gauls were 'all sworn brothers', while in the 18th century Sir Ewen Cameron of Lochiel boasted that his clan was 'all gentlemen'. The middle class was composed of free men who worked the land and had the right to bear arms when called upon, known in Welsh as the *theog* or *alltud*, or the 'tacksman' of the Scottish clan system. Then came the commoners, who in medieval Irish and Hebridean society were legally forbidden from fighting. At the bottom were the slaves, who were important to the Picts; there was a Dalriadan slave-girl at the Pictish court when St Columba visited it, Bede recorded the Picts enslaving Northumbrians, and St Patrick wrote to Coroticus to complain that he had been selling Irish Christians to the 'utterly evil and apostate Picts'.

In addition to this rigid class hierarchy there was the intellectual elite of the Druidic class. The Druids were not primarily 'priests'; while some performed a religious function, they also included historians, lawyers, judges, teachers, philosophers, poets, composers, musicians, astronomers, prophets, councillors, political advisers, craftsmen, blacksmiths and sometimes even kings and chieftains. As the intellectual caste they survived the coming of Christianity as the 'men of art', while Celtic clerics themselves were often called 'druids'.

Matrilinear succession

One unique aspect of Pictish society was that they are said to have practised matrilinear succession. Although difficult to prove, matrilinear succession appears to be shown in the Pictish king-lists, and was confirmed as the Pictish practice by Bede, as well as continuing in some Highland clans of Pictish descent.

Pictish silver neck-chains are around 50 cm long (20 in.), and weigh close to 2 kg (4.4 lb). (National Museums of Scotland)

Matrilinear succession does not mean Pictish queens ruled in their own right, but that the royal lineage followed the female blood-line. There are occasional instances of matrilinear succession in some insular Celtic tribes – Queen Maeve of Connaught's heir was her daughter; Vortimer inherited Gwent through the maternal line as a great grandson of Eudaf Hen the Old; and Boudicca's heirs were her daughters – but these are exceptional. Some have seen Pictish matrilinearity as a throwback to pre-Indoeuropean society, some as a deliberate form of proto-democratic policy, and others as a social response to particular economic circumstances shared by the Picts and people such as the Tongans and Masai. The Picts, of course, had their own beliefs about the practice.

The practical upshot of this form of succession was that the High King was chosen by election by the nobles out of a pool of potential rulers created by a complicated series of marriages between the seven royal houses. Pictish princes were raised from birth to be leaders, fully knowing only the best would be chosen by their peers, while Pictish princesses utilised different arrangements, including temporary 'handfast' marriages to visiting princes (in one Irish story Corc, son of Luigdech, has to kidnap his Pictish bride in order to take her to Munster), to bond the Pictish dynasties together. The result was that the Picts achieved a unique level of stability and political unity.

Map of the Pictish kingdoms. The Southern Picts consisted of (a) Fib, (b) Fortrenn, (c) Fotlaig and (d) Cirig, bounded by the Grampian mountains of 'the Mounth' to the north. The Northern Picts dwelt in (e) Ce, (f) Fidach and (g) Cait, and although the exact boundaries are unknown, it is likely Skye and Applecross were part of Fidach, and Orkney and the Shetlands ruled by Cait. Dalriada (h) was centred on Argyll, and Strathclyde (i) stretched into Cumbria, separated from Northumbria (j) by the Pennines. The British kingdom of the Goddodin (k) fell shortly after AD 600 and was absorbed by Pictland, Strathclyde and Northumbria. Galloway (l), bounded by the river Nith, was sometimes under Strathclyde's overlordship, sometimes Northumbrian, but always acted with independence.

An ancient British woman from John Speed's *Historie of Great Britaine* (1611).

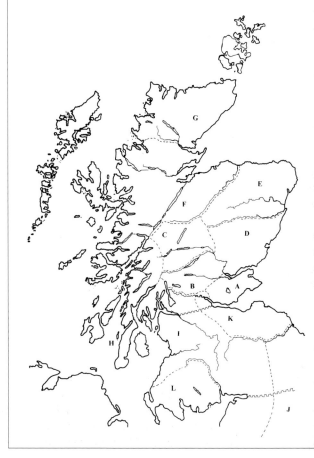

EDUCATION AND TRAINING

Noble sons were not raised by their birth parents, but sent for fostering by another family. It was considered a great honour to be entrusted with the upbringing of another's child, and in Ireland 'five hundred kyne and better' were sometimes given as gifts to ensure the fosterage of a great man's son. Fosterage was designed to create ties of brotherhood between two clans, and was practised by all Celtic societies, including the Picts – we know this because St Adomnan (St Columbus' biographer) mentions that Brude mac Maelchon had a foster-father.

The foster-father was responsible for providing a rounded education, which included physical, academic and artistic endeavours. Welsh, Irish and Highland sources paint a remarkably consistent picture of a young warrior's education, which must have applied to the Picts as well. The 'four and twenty games of the Britons' give a neat list of the skills a well-rounded Celtic warrior was expected to acquire, including 'Six Feats of Activity' (hurling weights, running, leaping, swimming, wrestling and riding), 'Four Exercises of Weapons' (archery or javelin throwing, sword, sword-and-buckler and quarterstaff), 'Three Rural Sports' (hunting, fishing and hawking), 'Seven Domestic Games' (such as poetry, musicianship, heraldry and diplomacy) and four board games.

Much of this education was entrusted to the Druids and bards, or later the Celtic Church. Although there was a strong emphasis on eidetic memory, the Christian Picts knew how to write ogham, and there are references to 'old books of the Picts', so there is no reason to believe they were any less literate than their neighbours; a sword-chape from Shetland is even inscribed in Latin with 'In the name of God the highest', and the name of the owner, 'Resad son of Spusscio'.

While intelligence and learning were highly valued, the martial arts were the first priority. Training began young; the Scots Highlanders began at age ten, the ancient Irish at seven. Several customs recorded in Wales, Scotland and Ireland show how important warfare was, even from childhood – for example, the right hand of the child would be left unblessed at Christening so that 'unhallowed blows could be struck upon the enemy', and even the first meat that a child received was served on the point of a sword.

Training in arms was systematic and sophisticated, and the Irish sagas contain a detailed syllabus of the *chleas* or 'feats' which a warrior was expected to master. These involved feats of dexterity

A grim-faced Pictish horse-lord leads his troops into battle on the Dupplin Cross.

17

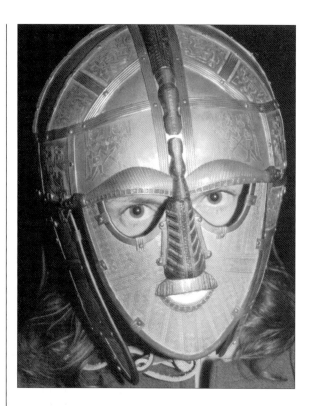

Among the very few pieces of possible Pictish helmets are fragments of embossed ornamental plates as found on 5th-7th century helmets such as the Sutton Hoo helmet. This reconstruction is by Warren Green.

(such as juggling swords), agility (such as th standing high jump or 'salmon's leap'), strengt (such as tossing the caber), voice (the stunnin 'hero's cry'), weapon handling, and finally th 'spear vault', where the champion would thrust spear butt-first into the ground and 'jump an perform on its point'. Many of these feats are als recorded in Highland folktales, indicating a lon standing tradition. Such feats could also be of grea practical value in combat, and for the Picts, wh generally fought unarmoured, the emphasis o agility and co-ordination would be vital. Some ide of their ability can be gained from the recruitin tests for the Irish *fianna*. 'In a trench, the depth o the knee, the candidate, with a shield and haze stick only, must protect himself from nine warrior casting javelins at him from nine ridges away. Give the start of a single tree, in a thick wood, he has t escape unwounded from fleet pursuers. So skilf must he be in wood-running, and so agile, that i the flight no single braid of his hair is loosed by hanging branch. In his course he must bound ove branches the height of his forehead, and stoo under others the height of his knee, withou delaying, or leaving a trembling branch behind. Without pausing in h flight he must pick from his foot the thorn it has taken up. In facing th greatest odds, the weapon must not shake in his hand.'

The young Pict would probably practise swordplay using sticks o 'cudgels', like later Highlanders, and the *Mabinogi* records how th Peredur practised with stick and shield against one of his cousins 'unt his eyebrow sagged down over his eye and the blood ran in streams'. Th Pictish warrior would be expected to master a variety of comba arts, including sword, single-handed axe and spear, alone and i combination with a buckler, two-handed spear, two-handed axe, dagge fighting and wrestling.

Games were an important tool for developing the skills needed fo survival on the battlefield. Games like shinty, played throughout th Celtic world since the Iron Age, were considered ideal practice for fas moving mêlées typical of Celtic warfare, and at night strategy games suc as *brandab* were played to keep the mind sharp. However, the emphasi was primarily on field craft, agility and prowess in individual combat.

Most Pictish training would be done in the foster-father's househol learning skills and techniques from veteran fighters. If the warrior wa exceptionally talented, however, he might receive further training a special 'martial academies', and the Irish tales credited the Picts wit having the best teachers of all. In the 'Wooing of Emer', Cú Chulainn told, 'if he could go and visit Domnall Mildemail, the War-Like in th land of Alba, he would fight more marvellously still; while if he visite Scathach, the Shadowy One, and studied the Warrior's Art with her, h could beat any Hero in Europe'.

The feats taught by masters such as Domnall and Scatha were highl potent, practical moves. For example, when Cú Chulainn fights 'Cocha

ruibne, one of Scathach's soldiers, and a very hardened man…Cochar
ried his special tricks of battle, but Cú Chulainn parried them as if he
ad studied them his whole life'. Here, the 'special tricks' are probably
dvanced techniques of swordsmanship.

Upon reaching adulthood the warriors would be required to give
ublic proof of both their valour and skill at arms, usually by
articipating in a raid and returning with some kind of trophy. The
liddle Irish 'Fitness of Names' states 'each young man of theirs [Ulster]
ho first took up arms would enter the province of Connacht on a foray
r seek to slay a human being', a custom still recorded in 17th-century
cotland. This ancient Celtic custom of headhunting for trophies also
ppears to have been practised by the Picts under at least some
ircumstances; on several occasions the Picts are recorded as beheading
efeated enemy leaders, a severed head is carved between two raven-
asked figures on a stone from Papil, Shetland, while piles of severed
eads are clearly depicted on the battle-face of Sueno's Stone.

ictish warrior bands

he fully trained Pictish warrior was part of a noble elite, and the right to
ear arms was the duty and privilege of the aristocracy. The warrior would
e a proud, boastful and confident professional fighter. Several Pictish
ones show war bands, and there appear to have been two classes of soldier
epicted: the mounted horse-warrior and the spear-armed infantryman.
owever, determining the exact structure of Pictish warrior bands is
ifficult from the available evidence.

The young Pictish warrior would
im to join a king's war band, and
xpect to receive hospitality, arms
nd treasure in return for service.
hey were not exactly mercenaries,
ut adventurous young nobles who
ffered their military skill to any
ader who rewarded them with fine
eapons, mead, feasts and praise
om the bards. Warriors earned
eir living by bearing arms, and
thenaeus quotes one old Celtic
ero as saying, 'My pointed spear, my
harp sword, my glittering shield are
y wealth and riches; with them I
lough, with them I sow, and with
em I make my wine; whoever
are not resist my pointed spear, my
harp sword, and my glittering
hield, prostrates himself before,
nd adores me as his lord and king'.

These sentiments still underlay
6th-century Celtic society, when
ohn Major wrote (rather less
ympathetically) that the High-
anders, 'delight in the chase and a
fe of indolence; their chiefs eagerly

Dark Age Celtic weaponry.
(a) Small Irish shield boss, Lagore.
(b) Arrowheads from Buiston, Ayrshire.
(c) 'Fire arrow' head from Dumbarton.
(d) Irish ribbed spearhead, Co. Offaly.
(e) 6th century British spearhead.
(f) Scottish javelin head, Dunadd.
(g) British javelin head, Buiston.
(h) Irish axe head, similar to those on Pictish carvings.
(i) Romano-British *spatha* hilt.
(j) Hilt from Co. Antrim, Ireland. The pommel bears some resemblance to the Norries Law sword.
(k) & (l) Typical wide-bladed Irish swords.

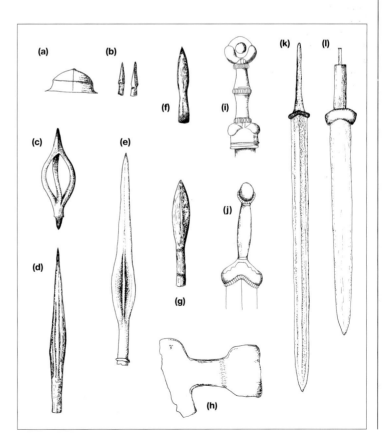

follow bad men if only they may not have the need to labour; taking no pains to earn their own livelihood, they live upon others, and follow their own worthless and savage chief in all evil courses sooner than they will pursue an honest industry'.

The primary military unit in Dark Age Celtic society was the band of mounted warriors who served the king. Caesar called them *equites* and in Wales they were called the *teulu* ('family'). Ireland had several such fraternities, of which the 'Red Branch' of Ulster is the most famous and distinguished, but others recorded in the Irish annals include the *Clanna Morna*, *Clana Baoisgne* and *Clanna Deagha*; the frequency of the word clanna in these titles indicates the importance of kinship. Others had more colourful names, such as the 'Men of the Lion', 'Men of the Green Swords', 'Men of Snow', 'Knights of the Calf' and, in Munster, the 'Knights of the Golden Collar'. The last group derived their name from a golden chain worn around the neck, like the torc that was indicative of status throughout Celtic Europe. Identical fraternities must have existed among the Picts, as at least ten massive silver neck-chains inscribed with Pictish symbols have been found throughout Scotland: these must have originally hung around the neck of campaigning horse-warriors. The fact that most have been found outside Pictish areas no doubt marks a sorry end for the original owners.

A Pictish war-band accompanied by war dogs, on a stone from Du[...]

An alternative to serving in a king's troop was to join a mercenary band where a young warrior could gain experience and accumulate wealth. In Ireland these bands were known as the *fianna*, and it was expected that noble sons would spend their youth in such a band as part of their education: it was even said 'every one is a *fian*-member until he comes into an estate'. Several years of service as a *fian* might even be necessary before the young warrior was considered worthy of joining a king's war band.

The understandable desire to segregate sexually mature, unmarried males from the rest of society has close parallels in many other tribal systems, and was an ancient Celtic practice; the historian Polybius describes a group called the *Gaesatae,* and the Gundestrup Cauldron features a row of beardless, spear-armed youths. In Wales they were known as *cantrefs,* and the medieval Gaels called them *ceathernach,* anglicised as 'kern' in Ireland and 'cateran' in Scotland.

The *fianna* were bound closely together as a pagan warrior cult, and when a new warrior joined he would undergo an initiation ceremony and undertake solemn oaths. Irish monks condemned them as the 'sons of death' and recorded that the *fian* made a 'vow of evil' and wore *diabolo instinctu* or 'diabolical marks', suggesting warrior tattoos like the Picts. The *fian's* oath of fealty was to their own chiefs, who were considered kings in their own right, and like other sub-kings were theoretically answerable to the High King.

The Fell pony, an ancient breed that is probably the large, heavyset horse shown on some Pictish stones.

Service in the *fianna* was a noble calling and a social service, and the new recruit was obliged to forswear the usual rights of compensation in case of death. Irish tales portray the *fianna* acting as a cross between the High King's paramilitary police force and a wandering band of 'knights errant', who were in high demand to provide military services for clans that did not have a 'Red Branch' of their own. When they were not needed the *fianna* supported themselves by hunting in the forests, and their life in the wilderness was often compared to that of wolves, and called 'wolfing' in the Irish annals. The Roman Marcellinus seems to refer to similar groups in the mid-4th century when he recorded that 'the Attacots warlike band, and the Scots, wandering up and down, committed great depredations'.

In Ireland, the presence of *fianna* bands can be tracked archaeologically by the presence of *fulacht fiadh* or *fulacht fian,* pre-prepared stone-lined cooking sites scattered throughout the wilderness for hunting bands to use as needed. In Scotland any such traces have long since been obliterated, but hunting was clearly an important part of Pictish noble life, and the extremely rich body of *fianna* lore in Highland folk tradition would seem to suggest that such bands existed in early medieval Scotland. However, their position in Pictish society is uncertain. 'Wolfing' was not an easy life, and the Irish *fianna* often drifted into brigandage, but there is no indication of widespread brigandage or instability in Pictland. It seems likely that inexperienced Pictish warriors had their service tied to particular clans or lords, rather than acting as freebooting mercenaries.

In times of crisis Celtic armies were augmented by foot soldiers provided by the lower ranks, who owed a certain amount of military service to their local rulers. Members of this class also provided the warrior's full-time servants, popularly known as 'ghillies'. Records of Pictish musters have not survived, but 12th-century Scotland retained a system which had its root in older tribal customs, and may provide some clues. The 'free service' was owed by freeholders, including the nobility, who were expected to have some amount of armour and to be mounted (everyone who possessed land had to keep at least one horse), while the 'Scottish Service' consisted of the peasantry, who had to present themselves twice a year, armed with bow, spear or axe. Although not professional warriors, the lower classes of Celtic society took the privilege of bearing arms seriously; in the 13th century Gerald of Wales wrote that his countrymen were

> entirely bred up to the use of arms; for not only the nobles but all the people are trained to war, and when the trumpet sounds the alarm the husbandman rushes as eagerly from his plough as the courtier from his court…they anxiously study the defence of their country and their liberty; for these they fight, for these they undergo hardships; and for these willingly sacrifice their lives; they esteem it a disgrace to die in bed, and honour to die in the field of battle…In time of peace the young men, by penetrating the deep recesses of the woods and climbing the tops of mountains, learn by practice to endure fatigue through day and night; and as they meditate on war during peace they acquire the art of fighting by accustoming themselves to the use of the spear and by inuring themselves to hard exercise.

These sentiments were echoed in 1250, when an Englishman wrote;

> The londe Scotia hath the name of Scottes that there dwelle. The nem are lygthe of harte, fiers and couragious on theyr enmyes. They love nyghe as well death as thraldome, and they account it for slouth to dye in bed, and a worshyppe and vertue to deye in a felde fyghtynge agynst enmyes.

APPEARANCE AND EQUIPMENT

Only a few fragmentary remains of Pictish military equipment have survived, from which very little can be concluded. The most complete find was the Norries Law Horde, a rich grave of a 5th-century Pictish warrior discovered in Fife in the early 19th century, which contained a large amount of silver: it was sadly destroyed for its bullion value. Fortunately, the visual records of Picts on their carved stones have left a detailed record of their appearance.

Pictish costume. (a) A shepherd wearing deeply pleated material perhaps a *leine* or belted plaid. (b) Two axemen grappling, wearing simple short tunics, from Glamis Manse. Such tunics are the most commonly depicted form of Pictish costume. (c) A cowled Pict with baggy shorts, from St Vigeans. (d) *David* from the St Andrews Sarcophagus, wearing what appears to be a belted plaid. Although the sarcophagus is unusual, the horseman matches closely with other Pictish carvings, so it can be argued that *David* is based on a contemporary Pictish shepherd as well.

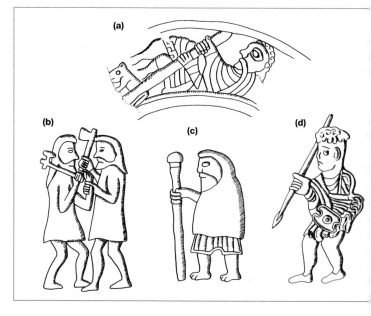

Clothing generally consisted of knee-length tunics, made from wool, linen or flax, often with a mantle, hood or cloak over the upper body. Bare legs seem to have been the norm, and Bede referred to the Picts as 'redshanks', an insult still used centuries later against bare-limbed 17th-century Highlanders. Bare feet were also common, although several leather shoes have been recovered. Several carvings appear to show belted plaids, or robes of deeply pleated material. No doubt a variety of colours were used, and woollen tartan was available, as shown by the 'Falkirk tartan', a fragment of material found near Falkirk and carbonated to AD 235. The Irish legend, *The Destruction of Da Dergas Hostel*, contains a brief description of three exiled warriors from Pictland, and describes their costume as three short black cowls about them reaching to their elbows: long hoods were on the cowls'. One such hood has been preserved on Orkney, and they are depicted on several Pictish stones.

Hairstyles among the Celts were often important outward marks of rank. Welsh warriors wore moustaches and short or even shaved heads 'for ease of running through thickets', while the Irish cut, outlawed by Henry VIIII, was 'shorn or shaven above the ears' with 'long hair (vulgarly called glibs) which hang down to the shoulders hiding the face... and this

A rare Pictish hood from Orkney. (National Museums of Scotland)

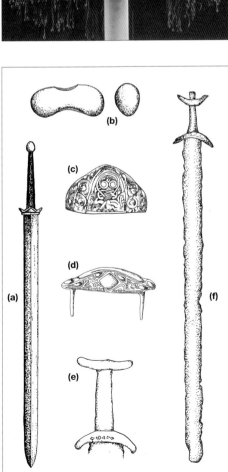

Fragmentary remains of Pictish swords.
(a) Possibly Pictish blade, 3rd century.
(b) Bone quillon and pommel from South Uist, perhaps 4th century.
(c) Silver pommel from the Norries Law horde, 5th-6th century.
(d) Bronze sword pommel from Cubin Sands, Moray, 6th-7th century.
(e) Possibly Pictish hilt, 9th century.
(f) Possibly Pictish sword, 9th-10th century.

hair being exceedingly long they have no use of cap or hat', and a style of thick moustache called a 'crommeal'. Pictish effigies generally indicate long hair, sometimes with moustaches and pointed beards, and the 6th-century Romano-British historian Gildas stated 'they were readier to cover their villainous countenances with hair than their private parts and neighbouring regions with clothes'.

Arms and armour

No armour can be discerned on Pictish carvings, except for one or two figures who might be wearing a quilted leather tunic. Archaeologically there are a few examples; there is a fragment of iron scale armour from Carpow in Perthshire, and the Norries Law Horde contained mail and 'rich coat of scale armour...of small-sized lozenge-shaped plates', with hooks for Roman-style *lorica squamata*, both of which were probably looted Roman gear. Even helmets are rare; the Aberlemno Stone shows horsemen wearing fairly typical Dark Age helmets with long nasals and cheek-plates, similar to the Coppergate, Benty Grange or Burgh Castle finds, but these are worn by the enemy, not the Picts. The Mortlach Stone shows a strange figure who appears to be wearing a helmet with horn crest, but only one fragment of a *spangenhelm* has ever been found apart from the lost 'silver' helmet of the Norries Law Horde.

Also in the lost horde was a long sword with a wide, round guard backed by a long quillon, and a small spherical pommel: this is often dismissed as 'fanciful'. Only a few fragments of Pictish swords have otherwise been found, including some globular 'Ultimate La Tene'-style bone and antler fittings associated with the brochs, and two decorated pommels similar to Anglo-Saxon ones. Pictish effigies show parallel-sided, broad-bladed swords with distinctly rounded tips, though length is hard to judge. The round ends are confirmed by the shape of surviving Pictish chapes, and indicates that Pictish swordsmanship was based on broad cutting strokes rather than thrusts.

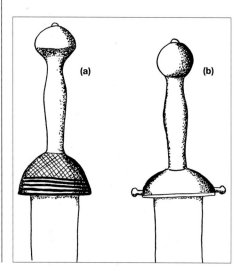

The curious 'Norries Law' sword, which was drawn from memory, may have originally been a *spatha*-like weapon, like this example from Gotland (a). (b) is a possible reconstruction.

Spears, both single- and two-handed, have broad heads; spear shafts were probably harvested directly from the forest, as the *Life of St Columba* records one Scot 'shaving the bark off a spear shaft with his own knife'. Other weapons depicted include distinctive single-handed axes, a two-handed battle-axe, and a short sax or knife. For most Celtic societies thrown spears or 'darts' were the primary offensive weapons, and are shown in the hands of Pictish horsemen on the Aberlemno stone – there is a clear parallel with the horsemen of *Y Goddodin*, who held 'spear shafts...aloft with sharp points' and 'cast spears of holly'. These were sometimes launched with the use of a thong, described as 'darts with variegated silken strings, thick set with bright dazzling shining nails, to be violently cast at the heroes of valour and bravery'. Overall, the arms of the Pictish warrior would thus appear to match closely with the description of the North British heroes from *Y Gododdin*, where 'they did not arm for battle, vigorous with spear and shield, sword and knife, any man who was better'.

Picts armed with bows are shown on the reverse side of the Dupplin Cross, the lost Meigle No.10 and on Sueno's Stone, indicating a long history to the strong tradition of

Highland archery. The Roman crossbow is also depicted on Shandwick and St Vigeans, and several 7th-8th century crossbow bolts and remains have been recovered. This weapon had a slow rate of fire and is only depicted in hunting scenes, but it is reasonable to presume that it would have occasionally found its way onto the battlefield as well. Some bows, such as the one on the Glenferness Stone, could be either type. The Picts are also said to have used packs of war dogs, which could inflict massive damage on an unarmoured opponent, and are depicted accompanying a Pictish war band on a carving from Dull.

Pictish horsemen carried round shields with circular bosses, held with a punch-grip, while the unarmoured Pictish infantry used small round or square bucklers. Contemporary Irish and British shields are described as 'lime-white', but some Pictish carvings show decorated shields that may indicate tooled leatherwork, like later Highland targes, and circular marks that may be decorations, rivets, or secondary bosses, a feature also found on Highland targes. In the Irish tale, *The Destruction of Da Dergas Hostel*, the equipment of the Pictish champions includes, 'Three black, huge swords they had, and three black shields they bore, with three dark broadgreen javelins above them; thick as the spit of a cauldron was the shaft of each.'

The black shields may indicate they were 'tarred' (widely used for both waterproofing and strengthening material by later Highlanders), while the swords and spearheads may have been left blue from the forge rather than polished, perhaps as protection against the Scottish weather; Dark Age north British poetry talks of 'blue blades', and Highland claymores were also described as 'great black blades'.

The Picts maintained a large number of hill forts, and some, like the 'royal fortress' at Burghead, contained structures such as a large well and a church, suggesting a large resident community. Most forts, however, were relatively small, built on rocky sites where a stone wall could follow the contours of the land and link natural outcrops together, a defensive strategy also popular with medieval Highlanders. Battles at such sites were commonly recorded and were important parts of Pictish warfare, although we know nothing about the methods used.

Pictish tattoos

The most striking aspect of Pictish appearance was the famous tattooing. The most direct references to Pictish tattoos come from the Roman poet Claudian, who spoke of 'this Legion, which curbs the savage Scot and studies the iron-wrought designs on the face of the dying Pict', and Tertullian, who implied that *stigmata Britonum* were the custom of both Britons

A selection of fantastic beasts. The commonly used 'sea elephant' (top left) is probably a dolphin.

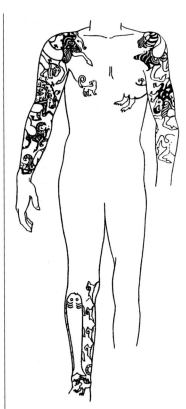
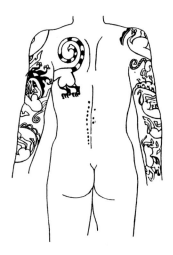

The Iron Age Scythian burials at Pazyryk have revealed tattooed warriors that give us an idea what Pictish tattoos may have been like.

and Picts. In 600 Isidore of Seville wrote, 'The race of Picts have a name derived from their bodies. These are played upon by a needle working with small pricks and by the squeezed-out sap of a native plant, so that they bear the resultant marks according to the personal rank of the individual, their painted limbs being marked to show their high birth'.

Because of the late date, Isidore's comments have often been dismissed as repetition of hearsay, but this is unlikely. Isidore did not have a word for 'tattoo', but his description is remarkably detailed and the use of the word *punctum* ('pricked') shows an understanding of the process. Spain was a favoured refuge for Britons fleeing their war-torn homeland, and in Isidore's day there was still an identifiable British community there so it is entirely possible he had the process explained to him first hand by Britons familiar with Pictish practices.

Even more interestingly, in 787 all forms of tattooing or *diabol instinctu* (the same 'diabolical marks' worn by the *fianna* and condemned by the Irish church) were explicitly forbidden by the Synod of Calcuth in Northumberland. The Pictish church joined with the Northumbrian church in 717, and from 768 the Picts fought a losing war against the Scottish king Causantin mac Fergus, who finally claimed the Pictish crown in 789. Northumbria was the only possible refuge for the defeated Pictish aristocracy, and an influx of tattooed warriors must have prompted the church to pass an edict against the practice, presumably because of its pagan associations. It thus seems likely that the Picts were a 'painted' people for their entire historical existence.

Interestingly, none of the authors mention a colouring agent, though Isidore comes closest. Woad is certainly possible, but 'Lindow Man' (the preserved remains of a 6th-century man, now in the British Museum) suggests that blue skin colouring could also be achieved by using a copper rich clay containing malachite or azurite. The 3rd-century historian, Herodian, implies that the Caledonians were painted with various colours, so blue may not have been the only colour achievable.

Animals appear to have been commonly used for personal decoration. 'They tattoo their bodies not only with likenesses of animals of all kinds, but with all sorts of drawings', wrote Herodian, and the 17th-century historian Duald MacFirbin, working from a now lost Gaelic source, stated 'the Cruithneach is one who takes the cruths or forms of beasts, birds and fishes on his face; and not on it only, but on his whole body'. Animals could provide tribal significance, a view supported by sites such as Burghead, which contains some 30 bull images. They could also be personal totems, where individual warriors might revere particular beasts for their speed or strength, fierceness or cunning.

The best clue as to what Pictish tattoos looked like are obviously the famous symbol-stones, which contain many depictions of animals and

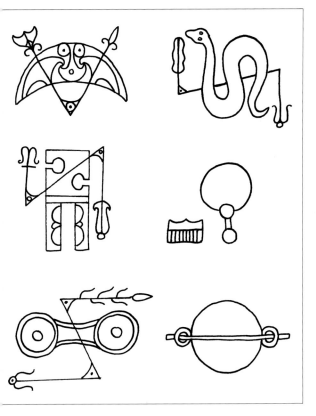

symbols. Pictish symbols are rich and varied, and the fact that they are complex and abstract, yet obviously had an instantly recognisable meaning for their audience, makes it certain they had a history of use and development long before they were first carved onto stone in the 6th century AD. It is possible that the symbols on Pictish stones started as personal decoration, and served much the same purposes. There is, however, no agreement as to the original purpose.

The earliest symbol-stones appear around the Moray Firth in the 6th century, and appear to be associated with the arrival of Christianity. While some symbol-stones may well be pre-Christian, the symbols continue in use in Christian cross-slabs from the early 8th century onwards. The symbol-stones themselves may have been proto-heraldic statements to impose a king's authority, memorials to the dead, or perhaps territorial boundary markers, or clan badges used to create unity between the Pictish dynasties. They may have expressed a combination of these things.

At least 50 different Pictish symbols have been recognised, although what the individual symbols mean is a matter of speculation. The 'serpent', for example, was symbolic of Druidic wisdom, but it also meant 'new life', due to its ability to shed its skin, and is used as such in the *Book of Kells*. The Pictish snakes could represent wisdom, the Druids, new life in the afterlife, or a 'new beginning' of marriage or peace between tribes.

selection of Pictish abstract ymbols. While there are many ieories, their meaning unknown.

ictish sculptors clearly had me access to illuminated anuscripts from Europe and ie Middle East depicting a ange of exotic beasts. Many ictish 'monsters' appear be North African creatures, ther copied from Church anuscripts or based on ie reports of Pictish ilgrims. Perhaps here) elephant, (b) ostrich,) crocodile, (d) camel,) perhaps a hippo, and a gnu?

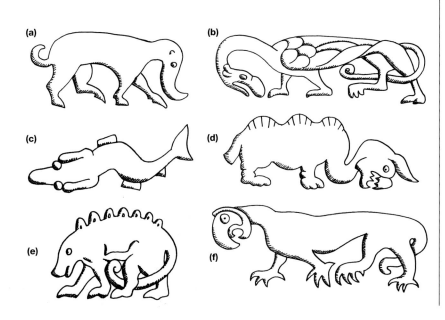

(a) (b) (c) (d) (e) (f)

Pictish tattoos were obviously of great cultural importance, and other tattooed societies may serve as models. Maori tattoos, for example, conveyed a great deal of information. One side of the face indicated the father's rank and bloodline, the other the mother's. Their tribe, the chiefs they had served, and their status and position within the tribe were also symbolised, as were their own achievements. The displaying of such information was vital for smooth inter-tribal relations, and has parallels in Celtic society, where rank and clan was indicated by clothing and hairstyle.

Did the Picts fight naked?

One controversial question about Pictish warriors is whether or not they fought naked. The popular perception is that this was the case, although many modern authorities, at pains to distance the Picts from their barbarian reputation, are more sceptical. There are certainly many Roman references to early Celts and Britons fighting naked, particularly the Caledonians, who are pictured naked on several Roman carved slabs, and of whom Herodian wrote, 'They are ignorant of the use of clothes…they tattoo their bodies not only with likenesses of animals of all kinds, but with all sorts of drawings. And this is the reason why they do not wear clothes, to avoid hiding the drawings on their bodies'.

None of this necessarily applies to the Picts, but Gildas, a 6th-century contemporary of the Picts, makes several direct references to the continuation of the habit, such as 'there was no respite from the barbed grappling irons flung by their naked opponents'.

While Gildas might not have portrayed the Picts in the most favourable terms, the Picts also seem to depict themselves naked on a number of stones. Those from Collessie, Balgavies and Rhynie closely resemble the ancient Caledonians shown by the Romans on the nearby Antonine Wall, and probably do not depict contemporary Picts. However, those from Eassie, Shandwick and St Andrews are Picts, and appear to be naked; although weathering may have removed details of clothing, it could not have removed their tunics to reveal the bare legs underneath.

These images would support Gildas' claim that the Picts did, after all, fight naked, although it is equally probable that it was the exception rather than the rule. Celtic societies generally frowned on public nakedness, and the Romans wrote of the Galatians (the Celts who inhabited Southern Turkey) that 'their wounds were plain to see because they fight naked and their bodies are plump and white since they are never exposed except in battle'.

Fighting naked was not an act of wanton bravery, but an invocation to divine protection, perhaps connected with the magical symbols painted on their bodies. There were also some practical reasons for fighting unencumbered with clothing, as naked bodies were harder to grapple in close combat, and a wound on bare skin was less likely to become infected than a wound rubbed by a dirty cloth. For such reasons many cultures around the world have traditions of duelling bare-skinned, and even Roman gladiators fought wearing only a helmet, vambrace and loin-cloth. It is interesting to note that the 'naked' Picts from Shandwick and St Andrews appear to be involved in duels, and it could well be that nakedness was – or became – restricted to such formal encounters.

It is also worth remembering that the psychological aspects of warfare were extremely important to all Celts, and the effect of a tartling physical appearance, particularly on a more reserved enemy ivilisation, was well understood. Naked warriors were intimidating in heir abandon, and an army of naked, heavily tattooed Picts would ertainly have been an arresting sight.

PICTISH SPIRITUALITY

The pagan Picts followed a broadly similar religion to other Celtic peoples, overseen by the Druids. While there is little concrete information on Pictish religious practices, the general flavour of Pictish beliefs is well recorded through the eyes of Irish churchmen such as St Columba and his biographer St Adomnan in the 6th and 7th centuries.

Like other pagan Celts, the Picts believed in a pantheon of gods and a supernatural 'otherworld', and an imaginative and colourful mythology permeated every aspect of Pictish life. It was a world where rivers and trees were sacred, where islands were rocks cast by giants, and

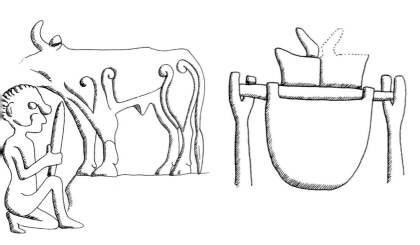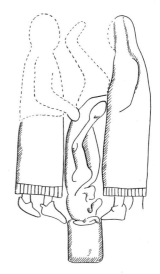

A Pictish bull sacrifice (left) and two images of human sacrifice, from Glamis Manse and St Vigeans.

here every well had sprung up from the touch of a saint's staff. The Irish missionaries regarded the Picts as particularly superstitious, and Adomnan recorded that, 'when the blessed man [St Columba] abode for some days in the kingdom of the Picts, he heard a rumour spread among the heathen people concerning another fountain, which the stupid folk reverenced as a god'.

Magic was extremely important; the Druids at Brude mac Maelchon's court were described as *magi*, and strenuously opposed Columba's efforts with curses and incantations, while the king was deeply impressed by St Columba's own magical signs. The Picts also seem to have had a deep connection with the animals that shared their land. Animal symbolism was obviously important, and it has often been remarked that the Pictish sculptors captured a spark of life in their animals that they rarely achieved with their human subjects.

Encounters between the Pictish Druids and the first Christians were sometimes hostile, but in general Pictish society underwent a peaceful transition to Christianity. St Ninian began conversion of the Southern Picts round 450, and in 486 St Darlugdach, Abbess of Kildare, was granted land at Abernethy by the Southern Pictish king Nechtan. By the time St Columba began his mission to the Northern Picts in 565 the Southern Picts 'are said to have abandoned the errors of idolatry long before this date and accepted the true faith'. Iona's speedy success with the Northern Picts was probably due to the ambition of Brude mac Maelchon to become king of both kingdoms – he needed a single religion to unite his people.

Like most early churchmen, St Columba usually sought to sanctify rather than extirpate native traditions, and when he came across phenomena such as a Pictish sacred spring he would bless it so that 'from that day the demon separated from the water'. The Pictish church, like other Celtic churches, achieved a tolerant synthesis with Druidic spirituality and local superstition. The survival of headhunting has already been noted, and it is clear that the Picts continued to believe in the magical power of symbols and animals. Divination through the 'second sight' was probably as important to Pictish society as it was to later Highlanders, and small painted charm-stones, similar to those used by Highlanders, are a common Pictish artefact.

One surviving link with Pictish beliefs may be that of the 'horse whisperers', practitioners of ancient craft that is said to have originated with the Picts or in the north-east. 'Horse whisperers' once formed a legendary elite among farm workers, and used several arcane methods to control and manipulate their animals. A low, whispering mumbling in the horse's ear 'in their own language' and the use of body language was combined with spells, potions, and equine aromatherapy. Repellent or 'jading' scents, such as a dead mole or bracken spores, could cause a horse to stop dead, and aromatic 'drawing' oils, involving oregano, rosemary, cinnamon, fennel and ginger, were used to neutralise 'jaders' or calm difficult horses. Such secrets could confer great advantages if, for example, horse whisperers managed to distribute 'jaders' across the path of the enemy cavalry.

Rhynie Man is a tonsured figure who may be a local warrior-saint, perhaps St Columba himself. His two-handed battle-axe resembles that of the Sutton Hoo find.

Pictish art is at its best when depicting animals, indicating a close observation of the natural world, with both reverence and the practical eye of the hunter.

30

Pictish stones also record images of sacrifice, which was clearly an important part of Pictish rites. There is one bull sacrifice, a custom recorded as late as the 17th century in the Highlands. Even more remarkably there are two carvings of human sacrifice, apparently by drowning in a cauldron. This practice is confirmed by references in the *Annals of Tigernach* to the Picts drowning enemy leaders in 734 and 739. Human sacrifice was widespread in the Celtic world, and a Briton named Odran even offered himself as a foundational sacrifice for St Columba to chase away the demons from Iona. The victims of ritual execution were usually criminals or prisoners of war; Bede recorded that following the battle of Dunnichenin in AD 685, 'many of the English at this time were killed', and Sueno's stone also depicts ritual beheadings following a battle. Although the Irish church abhorred human sacrifice, the Picts apparently retained a ritual manner of execution.

Pictish burials also provide evidence of Pictish religion, with cemeteries of long stone-lined cists, oriented east-west. Unlike earlier burials there are no grave-goods, indicating the graves were probably Christian, though the orientation of the bodies with the head to the west (the direction of the Celtic Otherworld) indicates a strong survival of pagan folk-belief as well. The Pictish church was never integrated in the Irish church, and tended towards alignment with Rome rather than Iona, probably due to the early efforts of St Ninian. In 717 the Pictish king Nechtan finally brought the Pictish church into communion with Rome and expelled the Columban monks 'across the spine of Britain'.

The way of the warrior

All Celtic warriors were proud and boastful, and extremely concerned with outward appearances. They loved the external trappings of wealth and privilege, as Pictish tattoos and silver jewellery testify, but it was more important to appear courageous and honourable. Because of this, they were prone to swagger and exaggerate. Emer describes herself to Cú Chulainn as 'Tara among women, fairest of maidens, a paragon of chastity', while Cú Chulainn boasts that 'At my weakest, I'm a match for twenty. A third of my strength is enough for thirty…Warriors avoid the battlefield for fear of me, and whole armies flee before me', to which Emer nonchalantly replies 'Not bad for a boy'.

A Pictish concern with honour and bravery would perhaps explain their lack of armour and even helmets. Fighting unarmoured was a deliberate choice by the Picts, who would certainly have had access to excess amounts of leather for *cuir bouilli*, and were sophisticated and capable metalworkers. The motivation may have been similar to that for fighting naked, in that it proved the warrior's courage and invoked the protection of the gods, or God. This possibility is suggested by the attitudes of other Celtic warriors, such as at Caratacus' last battle in AD 50, where the Britons forewent 'the protection of breastplates or helmets', believing their shields were all the protection a warrior needed. At the battle of the Standard in AD 1138 the unarmoured Galloway tribesmen were initially placed at the rear of the Scottish formation. Regarding this as an insult to their valour, the Gallovidian chieftain declared 'I wear no armour, yet they who do will not advance beyond me this day', indicating that relying upon armour was seen as cowardly.

Pictish centaurs may be symbolic of horse-whisperers or an Epona cult. A supernatural origin is suggested in the Irish tale *The Destruction of Da Derga's Hostel*, where the 'Room of the Cupbearers' contains 'six men…Fair yellow manes upon them: green mantles about them: in brooches at the opening of their mantles. Half-horses are they, like Conall Cernach…Those are the King of Tara's six cupbearers…They will share prowess with any six in the hostel, and they will escape from their foes, for they are out of the elfmounds'.

All Celtic societies held the warrior in high social esteem, and they fought within a strict code of honour. Celtic folklore abounds in incidents where heroes, assailed by multiple opponents, are chivalrously attacked one by one – there was no glory or honour in simply swarming over an enemy. The Pictish choice of small bucklers and broad, cutting swords indicates that single combat also played a large part in Pictish military encounters, as this combination confers considerable advantages in duelling, but is far from ideal in large-scale battle. Sueno's Stone shows two figures, presumably champions, duelling with sword-and-buckler in front of the watching army, indicating a Pictish custom of single combat much like that recorded by the Romans amongst ancient Celts.

Despite such bravado, outsmarting a stronger enemy was considered perfectly honourable, and the Celts were not above resorting to trickery. For example, when the legendary Pictish warrior-woman Scatha went to war with her rival Aife, whom she 'dreaded as the hardest woman warrior in the world . . . Aife challenged Scathach to single combat. Cú Chulainn went up to Scathach and asked her what Aife held most dear above all else.

'Three things she holds most dear,' said Scathach. 'Are her two horses, her chariot and her charioteer.'

Cú Chulainn met Aife and fought her on the 'rope of feats'. Aife smashed Cú Chulainn's weapon. All she left him was a part of his sword no bigger than a fist.

'Look, oh look!' Cú Chulainn said, 'Aife's charioteer and her two horses and the chariot have fallen into the valley, they are all dead!'
Aife looked around and Cú Chulainn leaped at her and seized her by the two breasts. He took her on his back like a sack, and brought her back to his own army. He threw her heavily onto the ground and held a naked sword over her.'

The Pictish warrior was part of a close-knit unit, in which the clannishness of the Celts was at its most extreme, with the warriors living, eating, sleeping, fighting, killing and dying together. The respect a warrior won from a glorious death did, to some extent, mitigate the sorrow at their loss, but Dark Age British poetry indicates that the death of a beloved leader had an intense impact on the warrior's mind.

A head I carry in my cloak:
The head of Urien, generous ruler of his court.
On his white chest ravens glut themselves.

A head I carry in my hand:
The head of the pillar of Britain has been toppled.
My arm has become numb.
My breast beats.
My heart is broken.

This reverence for leaders stemmed from an ancient belief that the well-being of the chief or king reflected itself in the well-being of the

Caledonian tribesman, AD 200 (see plate commentary for details)

A

Scatha's school of war

B

Pictish boats

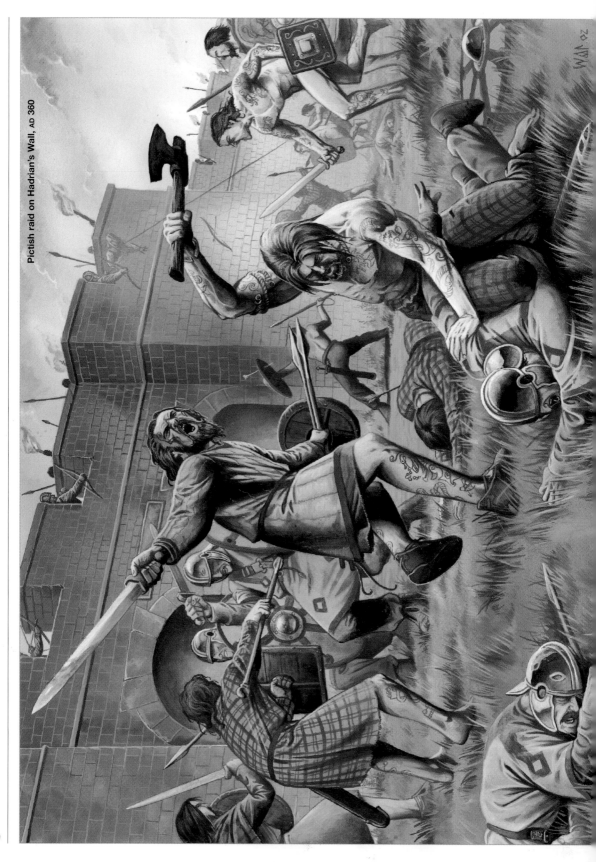

Pictish raid on Hadrian's Wall, AD 360

D

Pictish weaponry (see plate commentary for details)

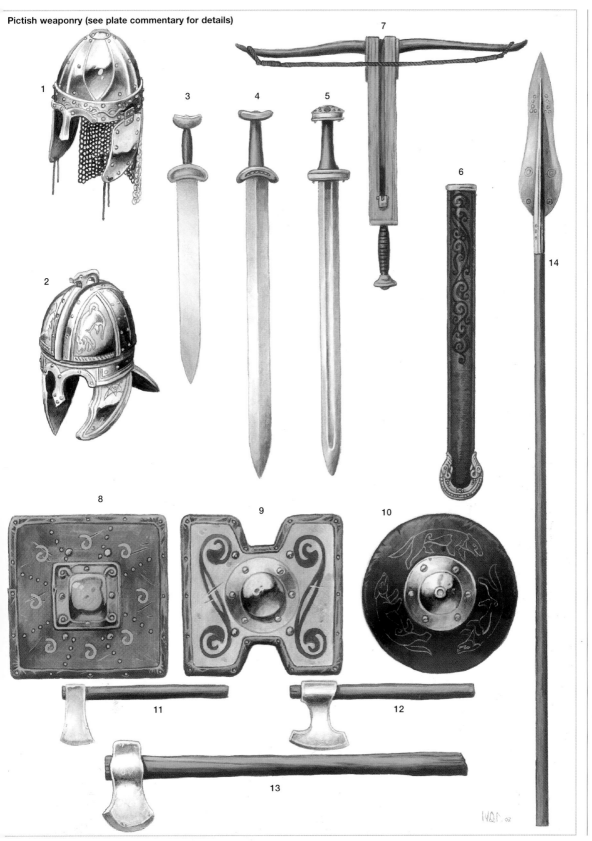

E

Pictish warriors, AD 690

F

Battle with Strathclyde, AD 744

H

land. If the king was in harmony with his duties then the land flourished, but if a king was unjust or neglected his obligations, this was reflected back on the land. In practice a king's rule was often judged by the state of his country, rather than the other way round, and the 'self-evident' proofs of the falsehood of a king were signs such as defeat in battle, dryness of cows or scarcity of corn. Aeden of Dalriada was removed from office early in the 7th century after he was defeated by the Angles at Degastan, and the Pictish king-lists indicate several instances where the Pictish nobles would seem to have removed a king.

THE HUNT AND THE FEAST

The everyday life of the Pictish warrior was one of relative luxury and leisure. The bulk of the Pictish population scraped by in small family groups, practising both cropping and herding in order to support the warrior aristocracy; the tribute collectors of the Pictish king Nechtan were noted in the Irish annals as being particularly unpopular.

The warriors based themselves around the nobles' hill forts and feasting halls, where they trained, played, feasted and hunted together. Pictish halls were large, rectangular wooden structures, though only the post holes and bedding trenches have survived, such as at Green Castle, Portknockie. Most individual dwellings were simple wattle-and-daub huts, though in the far north, stone was the normal building material.

Hunting was a important pastime for the Picts, and hunting scenes are depicted on many stones, such as those from Aberlemno, Fordoun, Hilton of Cadbol, Inchbrayock and Shandwick. Hunting expeditions served significant social and political purposes for the Pictish nobles and leaders, and although the meat was no doubt a welcome bonus, a Highland proverb noted that 'the chase is but a poor livelihood'. For free-living *fian*, however, hunting was not merely a pastime but a necessity.

The Picts hunted in different ways. Most scenes show spearmen on horseback, accompanied by horn-blowing servants and packs of hunting dogs, and occasionally women, depicted riding side-saddle. Big game included red deer, wolves, bears, wild boar and the fierce wild cattle of the Highlands. Not all hunts were conducted from horseback, however, and boar were also stalked with crossbows, a dangerous pastime that remains popular today in outback Australia.

Apart from hunting, banquets were the other most important social event. These might be held to celebrate the seasonal Celtic festivals of Samhain, Imbolc, Beltane and Lughnasad, or the many Christian holy days. Feasts would also be held before a major expedition against the enemy, or in celebration after a successful raid, battle or hunt. Feasts were ceremonially

A hunting scene from the Hilton of Cadboll stone. The woman is riding side-saddle, and is being followed by a short-tailed terrier, in contrast to the deerhounds bringing down the game.

important occasions. Seating arrangements depended upon the warriors' status, and a mistake might lead to a deadly duel or even an inter-clan war. Similarly, the greatest warrior would be entitled to the 'heroes' portion' of the meat, but might be challenged and have to prove his right to the joint in single combat. Gerald of Wales said that the Picts, like the Welsh, were 'immoderate in their love of food and intoxicating drink'. A Pictish king had access to wine imported from Gaul and the Mediterranean, honey-mead, probably whisky, and the legendary Pictish 'heather ale', all of which were generously supplied to ensure the grateful loyalty of his war band, as well as raise his own reputation and status in the eyes of the bards.

Feasting halls were important parts of the Pictish warrior's world. A clue as to their appearance is the 'Temple of Jerusalem' in the *Book of Kells*.

Feasts were not necessarily the rough, wild, drunken affairs that are often imagined. Tradition and custom had to be followed, fairness and self-restraint were admired as virtues, and a sense of humour and clever conversation were highly valued. The Pictish warrior would be expected to be shrewd and quick-witted, skilled in word-play, and in sarcastic and satirical humour, as Diodorus wrote of the Celts in the 1st century BC: 'When they meet together they converse with few words and in riddles, hinting darkly at things for the most part and using one word when they mean another; and they like to talk in superlatives, to the end that they may extol themselves and depreciate all other men. They are also boasters and threateners and are fond of pompous language, and yet they have sharp wits and are not without cleverness at learning'.

Poetry, music, dancing and storytelling were considered manly endeavours. During the feast the bards would sing and tell tales, celebrating the ancestry, courage and generosity of those who favoured

A boar hunt from St Vigeans. Three Pictish stones show the crossbow, and several fragmentary remains have been found.

them, and satirising those they disliked, who would then lose face and status in front of the assembled host. Music would be provided by instruments such as the *cruit* or *crwth*, an ancient type of lyre, the *clarsach* or harp, the *bodhran* (drum), *feadan* (whistle or flute) and Pictish triple-pipes. After the stories and songs, the evening would probably end with energetic dancing to Celtic reels.

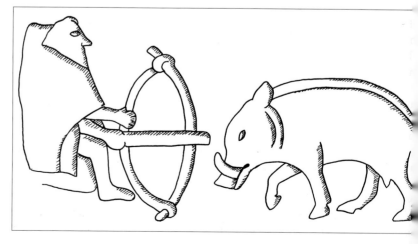

HE EXPERIENCE OF BATTLE

he raid

'here are no detailed descriptions of Picts in battle, but a considerable
mount of information can be gleaned simply on the basis of their
quipment. The choice of fighting unarmoured, with broad cutting
words and small bucklers, immediately suggests a preference for active,
•pen skirmishing warfare rather than the 'shield wall' favoured by the
.nglo-Saxons and Vikings.

The Picts went to war for a variety of reasons. Cattle-rustling was a
ime-honoured tradition, while ravaging enemy territory to exact tribute
·as well tried against the Roman Empire and
ontinued in later centuries. Inter-kingdom politics
lso played a role and Pictish alliances constantly
hifted; former enemies often became allies in the
uest for new territory or the defence of their own.

The Picts did fight large-scale battles, often with a
igh level of sophistication and success. However, the
nost common military activity was the raid, a short-
erm expedition whose main purpose was to collect
oot, cattle and slaves. Gildas described the Picts and
.cots of his own time as raiders who avoided set
,attle, 'wandering thieves who had no taste for war ...
n perfect accord for their greed for bloodshed'.

The raid held a special ritual significance, and
ould even be a legal requirement. The 'first
.dventure' of a young lord was an important occasion,
vhere tradition demanded he raid cattle from an
nemy to prove himself fit for command, and young,
.ntested warriors vied for positions in the leader's
etinue. As late as 1695 Martin Martin recorded the
·ractice in the Highlands, identical to the *crech rig* or
king's raid' practised in ancient Ireland.

Raids could have several objectives, such as
.eadhunting, cattle-rustling, blackmail or kidnapping,
he collection of slaves, or plain old looting and pillaging. The choice of
argets for the Picts was limited – while there are occasional Pictish civil
vars and instances of piracy by the Orkneymen, they are conspicuous by
heir rarity, and most raiding would have been against foreigners. This
neans that Pictish raids were probably fairly substantial expeditions, like
he mythic 'Cattle Raid of Cooley', with participants counted in the
nundreds or more.

Surprise was a vital element, so the raiding party would often move
t night. They would agree on signals and a plan of action, often leaving
. party behind to secure vital fords or prepare an ambush in case of
·ursuit. Against Roman Britain careful planning and a substantial
:entralised army would have been necessary to deal with the Legions,
.fter which the raiders would have free reign. In the post-Roman period,
·owever, there was always a chance of interception by an enemy
var band, so speed was essential. Unnecessary bloodshed was avoided
·here possible, to minimise revenge attacks. The most difficult part was
·rotecting the booty on the march back home, as even a successful raid

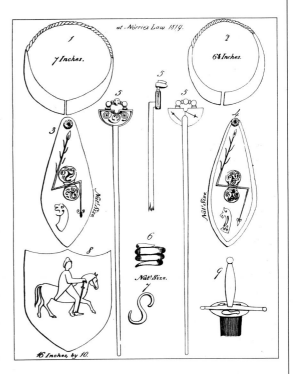

**Objects from the Norries Law
Horde. 1 and 2 are obviously
torcs, and 6 may have been
an armband. The sword (5),
drawn from memory, is startling
in its design but should perhaps
not be dismissed as fantasy.**

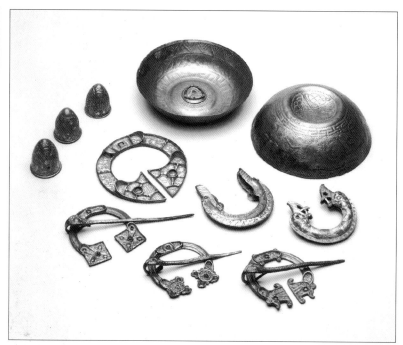

could be quickly reverse[d] if enemy horsemen overtoo[k] the slow-moving cattle-train.

A profitable raid woul[d] result in wealth for the leade[r] who would then distribute th[e] spoils generously among h[is] followers. The importance [of] the raid to the maintenanc[e] of Celtic society is more full[y] explained in Warrior 30, *Celt[ic] Warrior 300 BC – AD 100.*

The Pictish army

The size of armies of th[e] Pictish period was relative[ly] small. On the founding [of] Dalriada, for example, 'thre[e] times fifty men passed over i[n] the fleet with the sons of Erc[,] while the Gododdin forc[e] numbered 300 hand-picke[d]

Sumptuous Pictish silverwork from the St Ninian's Horde, Shetland. Metallurgical analysis has shown that most Pictish silver was reused Roman metal. (National Museums of Scotland)

men. In the Welsh Triads one of the 'Three Invincible Armies of th[e] North' was the 'three hundred spears of the Sons of Coel', and Cunedda['s] 'nine hundred horse' was enough to drive out an entire population.

In addition to the professional warriors, however, the king could ca[ll] upon reserves from the lower classes, and sophisticated mechanism[s] existed for assembling the national levies. The Dalriadan *Senchus Fer [us Alban* records that the Scottish sea-muster was 1,000 'rowing benches', eac[h]

The Monymusk reliquary or *breachbannach* of St Columba, a shrine of Pictish workmanship that brought victory at Bannockburn.

f which might have represented two or three oarsmen – bout the same as the Campbells or MacDonalds were ble to put into the field in the 18th century. The Picts ere able to call on the mounted war bands of seven ingdoms for cavalry and tribal levies for infantry, in ddition to the independent *fian* bands who theoretically erved the High King. The High King of the united Picts as thus probably the most powerful man in Britain, and ould well have assembled over 10,000 fighters if ecessary.

Before the army set out there would be a feast for he heroes, where meat and drink would be in plentiful upply. Not only did this instil a sense of camaraderie mong the band, but it indebted each warrior to the ing, and thus spurred him on to great feats in order to earn his mead'. There might be sacrifices and eligious services to gain the blessing of the gods or Jod, as well as divinations – prophesy was an important art of Celtic spirituality, and it is likely that many ecisions would be made on the basis of the seers' isions. A prophesy for success would leave the army nthusiastic and confident; an unfavourable reading night not be enough to abort the expedition, but ould certainly have a negative psychological impact.

When on campaign the Pictish army could move swiftly without the eed for a large baggage train. Herds of cattle were simply driven along nd slaughtered as needed, or stolen from the enemy. The tradition in nedieval Ireland and both Lowland and Highland Scotland was for each arrior to carry a bag of oatmeal which could be fried with blood or ater, while the meat was boiled in the hides of the slain cattle, so there as not even a need for cumbersome pots. A description of an Irish osting records how they fed 'upon herbs and roots, their drink is beef roth, milk, and whey. They let their kine bleed, which being cold they ake in a pan, and spread upon bread. In haste they squeeze out the lood of raw flesh and feed upon it without farther dressing, which they oil in their stomach with Aqua Vita'.

reparation for battle

s battle approached there was a great deal of ritual to be observed. ccording to Tacitus, prior to the battle of Mons Grampius the union of he various Caledonian tribes was ratified by solemn rites and sacrifices, nd the Pictish use of sacrifice makes it likely that similar rituals were bserved. As late as the 13th century the prince of Galloway made a imilar mystical bond with a cateran (unmarried adult male) captain amed Gilleruth. 'They made an unheard of covenant, inventing a kind f sorcery, in accord with certain abominable customs of their ancient orefathers. For all those barbarians and their leaders...shed blood from he pre-cordial vein into a large vessel...and they stirred and mixed the lood after it was drawn; and afterwards they offered it mixed to one nother in turn and drank it as a sign that they were henceforward ound in an indissoluble, and as it were consanguineal covenant, united n good fortune and ill, even to the sacrifice of their lives'.

Pictish helmets were probably of the same basic post-Roman ridge or *spangenhelm* design found elsewhere, such as the 7th-century 'Pioneer helmet' from Northamptonshire. This reconstruction of the helmet is by Craig Sitch of Manning Imperial.

Another common custom was the creation of a cairn, commonly erected over Pictish graves; each warrior would bring a stone and place it in a pile, and afterwards the survivors would each remove a stone, leaving the remainder as a memorial to the fallen – an early description of the custom is found in the Irish narrative *The Destruction of Da Derga's Hostel*, an event which occurred in the early 7th century.

The king would be in charge of the overall battle-plan, and the formation would naturally depend upon the enemy being faced, whether they were British horsemen, Roman legionaries, a Saxon shield-wall or a fortified hilltop. The formation on the Aberlemno Stone indicates that the Pictish army was no mere mob, but would have been carefully deployed, taking into account factors of seniority and status as well as military considerations. By the 7th century the totem animal figures of the ancient Celts had, in Ireland, given way to proto-heraldic battle banners, and the Irish annals describe battles where 'every captain bore upon his standard his particular device or ensign'. If Pictish symbol-stones are indeed proto-heraldic devices, similar banners may well have been used, so each war band would be deployed under their own standard.

The place of the Pictish warrior within his or her unit would depend upon their status. The champions fought in the front line, with lower status warriors further back. As the lines formed up there would be a round of psychological warfare, where the Picts would attempt to intimidate the enemy; a champion might strip off to display his magical tattoos, whirl his weapons and perform 'feats' to impress the foe with his agility and skill, or lampoon the enemy and challenge them to single combat. Many Celtic warriors fought under the influence of 'battle madness', the *dasachtach* or *miri-cath* made famous by Cú Chulainn. While this could occur spontaneously under extreme stress, meditation techniques and narcotics such as henbane might also be used to deliberately achieve the *berserk* state of mind.

Of particular importance were the bards, who would encourage the warriors to emulate the glories of their ancestors, while calling down doom upon the enemy. Pictish bards appear on a number of stones, and were clearly as important to the Picts as they were to other Celts. In Welsh law the *bardd teulu* was required to sing *Vnbeinyaeth Prydain* (*The Chieftainship of Britain*) before battle, while the *brosnachadh catha* or 'incitement to battle' was a vital preparation for the Highland charge, and Highland bards were noted 'eulogising the fame resulting from a glorious death...as well as the disgrace attending dastardly conduct or cowardly retreat'. Sometimes these songs were prophetic, such as Taliesin's poem *The Battle of Argoed Llwyfain.*

The Viking *berserkers* and Celtic *fianna* shared a great many characteristics, including an association with wolves.
(a) A berserker from the Hebridean 'Lewis Island' chess set.
(b) A Norse warrior dressed in a wolf-pelt, from a 7th-century helmet plaque.
(c) Wolf-masked Picts from Kettins, Angus.
(d) Dog-headed figure from Mail in Shetland.

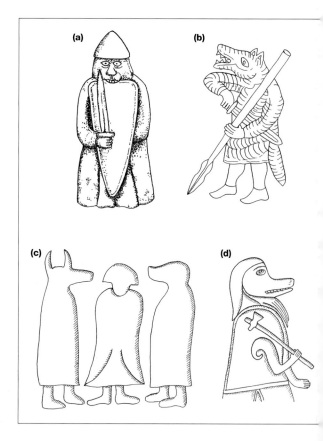

Let us carry our spearshafts over the mountain
And lift our faces above the ridge
And raise our lances over men's heads
And attack Fflamddwyn in the midst of his host
And slay both him and his companions.

Others were reminders of past victories:

Great sovereign, all high ruler
Refuge for strangers, a strong defender in battle
The English know this when they tell their stories -
Theirs was death, theirs was rage and grief
Their homes are burnt, their bodies are bare…

The bards did not fight, but carefully watched the deeds of the warriors; the slightest hint of cowardice would be recorded and immortalised in song and verse, and thus their very presence had a positive effect on the behaviour of each champion.

When the voices of the bards could no longer be heard, the musicians began to frighten the foe with a cacophony from their deafening war-trumpets. Rather than the ancient carnyx, most Pictish stones show long, straight trumpets or cow horns; the mouth of a looted 9th-century Anglo-Saxon blast horn was found at Burghhead, indicating Pictish use. The use of loud music to intimidate enemies in battle was an ancient Celtic custom, and even in the 14th century the Scots retained the practice, as the chronicler Froissart recorded. 'The Scots have a custom, when assembled in arms, for those who are on foot to be well dressed, each having a large horn slung round his neck, in the manner of hunters, and when they blow all together, the horns being of different sizes, the noise is so great it may be heard four miles off, to the great dismay of their enemies.'

Like the well-known tunes of the Highland war pipes, battle horns provided stimulus in battle, frightened the foe, and were also a means of signalling to the army, so the Pictish king could issue orders to his troops even over the din of battle.

Scottish deerhounds. These swift and powerful hunting dogs, along with the closely related Irish wolfhound, were famed throughout the ancient world, and are said to have been used as war dogs by the Picts.

Battle is joined

The purpose behind all these rituals was to 'psych up' the warriors for battle, which would probably have opened with a blinding Celtic charge. This is likely simply because neither the Pictish horsemen nor the unarmoured foot soldiers, protected only by a buckler, were equipped for defensive warfare, and so the Picts would generally have preferred an open mêlée where their speed, agility and individual weapon skill could be put to best advantage. Parallels with the charges of the ancient Celts, and later the unarmoured tribes of medieval Galloway and the 18th-century Jacobite Highland clans are obvious.

However, there is also evidence that the Picts did not simply rush blindly into battle, but were capable of fighting in disciplined formations, waiting patiently for the right moment to attack, and carrying out complex large-scale manoeuvres. Dawn attacks are commonly recorded, which required good intelligence, careful planning and disciplined manoeuvring and positioning of troops. For example, around AD 460 the Picts and Dalriadans formed an alliance against the north British king Coel Hen. The medieval Scottish historian Hector Boece recorded the tradition that Coel invaded Galloway and Ayrshire and set up 'in a fortress prepared in advance'. A deserter from the Scottish forces betrayed the whereabouts of the Pictish and Scottish cattle, and Coel sent half his army off to capture them, after which he could besiege and starve the enemy. The Picts and Scots were alerted to this plan, divided their forces and launched an attack of their own:

> Fergus launched a surprise night attack on the British camp, killing the sentries and storming the rampart before Coil knew what was happening: then, while the Britons were trying to fight off the Scots, the Picts raised a terrible shout and suddenly attacked them from behind. Thus the Britons, barely awakened from sleep and unable to rally round their standards or their leaders, were routed. Some, concealed by the dark night, found

The Aberlemno Battle Stone has usually been assumed to represent the battle of Dunnichen in AD 685, and indeed the connection between them has become something of a modern myth, simply because Dunnichen appears, from a modern 'Celt vs. Saxon' viewpoint, as a particularly historic battle. However, the nasal-helmed foe are shown all mounted, just like the Britons of *Y Goddoddin*, while there is not a single recorded example of Anglo-Saxons in Britain fighting from horseback prior to 1052. This makes their identification as 'Northumbrians' extremely suspect. The slab itself is a 'Class II' Pictish stone and on art historical grounds is generally believed to have been erected in the mid-8th century, placing it in the reign of Oengus Mac Fergus, a successful warrior-king who could be expected to celebrate one of his own victories. It is likely that Aberlemno actually depicts the great Pictish victory over the Britons of Strathclyde in AD 744.

safety in flight: others, not knowing the country, wandered among twisting glens and steep drops until they were either hunted down or swallowed up by bogs.

A fragment of scale armour from Perthshire. (National Museums of Scotland)

The Aberlemno Stone provides some idea of Pictish tactics. In the upper strip a Pictish horseman with a sword is chasing an enemy who has thrown away his weapons. In the centre panel Pictish infantry stand in three ranks to face the oncoming cavalry; the front man has his shield ready and his sword raised, the second rank presents a long two-handed spear which protrudes to protect the front rank, with a shield strapped over his shoulder. The man in the third rank stands with his spear at rest until needed. In the bottom section, two horsed warriors charge each other throwing javelins. This battle, whatever it was, was a victory for the Picts as indicated by the dead mail-coated enemy who has become 'food for the ravens'. The horsemen above and below probably represent cavalry units flanking the main pike-block.

Most Dark Age armies, such as the Vikings and Anglo-Saxons, formed shield-walls with spear-and-shield, but the Pictish pike-block or *schiltron* as depicted would have been a superior anti-cavalry formation. The sword-and-shield men in the front rank not only gave the spearmen some protection from thrown javelins, but also fended off knife-men attempting to get in under the spears (one method the ancient Celts used to defeat similar Greek formations). The *schiltron* remained the primary Scottish formation for another 800 years, and featured prominently in both the Welsh Wars of Edward I and the Scottish Wars of independence.

The Eriskay pony.

Y Gododdin

One of the best descriptions of a Pictish-era battle is found in *Y Gododdin*, a poem by the 6th-7th century British bard Aneurin. *Y Gododdin* records a sortie by 300 of the most renowned warriors of the day from all Celtic Britain, including Picts, led by the king Mynyddawg Mwynfawr against the Anglo-Saxon stronghold at Catterick. Military actions at fortifications were common features in the wars between the Picts, Scots and Britons, so the warriors were probably not intimidated by Catterick's old Roman stone walls which were seven-and-a-half feet thick.

49

The champions of the Gododdin were all mounted, armed with swords, spears and javelins, and supremely confident. The epic poem transmits some of the personality of the Celtic heroes as they set out on the glorious expedition:

A man in might, a youth in years,
Courageous in battle
Swift, long-maned stallions
Under the thigh of a fine lad
Behind him, on the lean, swift flank
His target, broad and bright,
Swords blue and bright,
And hilts of goldwork.
There'll be not between us now
Reproach or enmity –
Rather shall I make you
Songs in your praise.

The northern Celts were determined to expel the Saxons, despite the formidable odds stacked against them, and Aneurin recorded the fury of the assault.

Wearing a brooch in the front rank, bearing weapons
    in battle,
a mighty man in the fight before his death day,
a champion in the charge in the van of the armies:
there fell five times fifty before his blades,
of the men of Deira and Bernicia a hundred score fell
    in a single hour.

He would sooner the wolves had his flesh than go to
    his own wedding,
he would rather be a prey for ravens than go to the
    altar,
he would sooner his blood flowed to the ground than
    get a due burial,
making return for his mead with the hosts in the hall.

The heroes of the Gododdin got their wish; the expedition was a disaster. The northern Celts were probably vastly outnumbered and ill-equipped for attacking such a strong fort, but the pre-battle drinking may also have had an effect. Aneurin wrote,

To Nudd, the son of Ceido
I loved him who fell at the onset of battle
The result of the mead in the hall and the beverage of
    wine.

The elite of the northern Celts were slaughtered and left to 'glut Black Ravens on Catraeth's walls', an image similar to that carved on the Aberlemno Stone. Of 300 warriors the only one who returned alive was

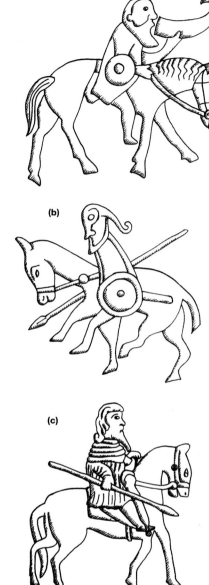

(a)

(b)

(c)

Most Pictish horses wear only a pad in the Irish fashion (a), and others appear to be bareback (b), although the Kirriemuir horsemen (c) appear to show a high saddle and stirrups.

the bard himself, who wrote this magnificent elegy as a lasting testimony to the doomed expedition:

> The men went to Catraeth with the dawn,
> their high courage shortened their lives.
> They drank the sweet yellow ensnaring mead,
> for a year many a bard made merry.
> Red were their swords (may the blades never be cleansed),
> and white shields and square-pointed spearheads
> before the retinue of Myynyddawg the Luxurious.

The aftermath of battle

If successful in battle the victorious Picts would pursue the defeated foe with eagerness and scour the battlefield for booty. The enemies' baggage and cattle would be seized, camp followers enslaved, the bodies stripped of jewellery and decapitated for trophies. Enemy leaders who were captured would be ritually sacrificed by beheading or drowning amid great ceremony. If the victory took place in enemy territory, the surrounding countryside could expect to suffer as well, with the inhabitants enslaved or driven out. Bede recorded such events following the Northumbrian defeat at Dunnichen, when 'many of the English at this time were killed, enslaved, or forced to flee from Pictish territory'. Technically, all the battlefield loot belonged to the king, who distributed the wealth among the survivors. There was generally a strict division of spoils, with the king eager to appear fair and generous in the eyes of both the bards and warriors.

If unsuccessful, the Pictish host would quickly melt away before the victorious enemy. Although there are plenty of instances where cornered Celtic warriors would fight bravely to the death, a retreat from a losing battle was not generally considered cowardly. Gerald says of the Welsh that 'although beaten today and shamefully put to flight with much slaughter, tomorrow they march out again, no whit dejected by their defeat or loss',

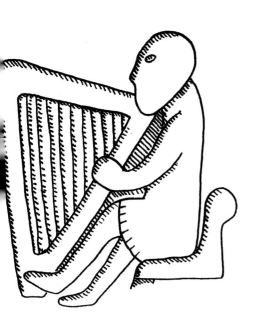

Pictish bards playing the harp, cruit and triple-pipes, which utilises didgeridoo-style circular breathing and is still played in Sardinia.

while the Highlanders had a proverb, 'better a good retreat than a bad stand'. The alternative was gruesome: in 672 Ecgfrith of Northumbria massacred a trapped Pictish army at Carron, and two rivers were so full of corpses 'so that, marvellous to relate, the Northumbrians, passing over the rivers dry-shod, pursued and slew the crowd of fugitives'.

Dark Age Celtic medicine was surprisingly sophisticated, and a wounded Pict had a relatively good chance of survival. The medics, part of the Druidic class, were knowledgeable in herbal lore and capable of reasonably sophisticated surgery such as amputations and trepanation. Tacitus noted that the Celts carried their wounded off the field even during battle, so the women could tend their wounds.

Win or lose, the deeds of the battle were recorded by the bards for posterity. They would praise the great warriors who had fallen, relate the heroic actions of the survivors, and compose plaintive dirges for the slain. If a warrior received the praise of a bard for some heroic deed, his status was significantly increased. Although no Pictish bardic material has come down to us (unless hidden within Highland folklore), the compositions of the contemporary northern British bards are poignant, especially when lamenting a slain hero or a bitter defeat. When King Urien of Rheged was assassinated, Llywarch Hen wrote,

This hearth, wild flowers cover it.
When Owain and Elphin lived
Plunder boiled in its cauldron…

This hearth, tall brambles cover it.
Easy were its ways
Rheged was used to giving…

This hearth, dockleaves cover it.
More usual upon its floor
Mead, and the claims of men who drank…

This pillar and that pillar there.
More usual around it
Shouts of victory, and giving of gifts.

Taliesin's elegy for Urien's son Owain reads,

When Owain slew Fflamddwyn
It was no harder than sleeping
Sleeps now the host of broad England
With the light in their eyes
And those who did not flee
Were braver than they had need

Owain punished them soundly
Like a pack of wolves after sheep
Splendid he was, in his many coloured armour,
Horses he gave to all who asked
Gathering wealth like a miser
Freely he shared for his soul's sake

The soul of Owain ap Urien
May the Lord look upon its need…

When the court of Cynddylan of Shropshire, 'the bright buttress of the borderland', was destroyed by the Saxons, Llywarch Hen lamented:

'Stand out maids, and look on the land of Cynddylan,
The court of Pengwern is ablaze;
alas for the young who mourn their brothers…

'The hall of Cynddylan is dark tonight,
Without fire, without bed;
I weep awhile and then fall silent…

'The eagle of Eli; loud his scream tonight,
Sated with gory drink;
the heart's blood of Cynddylan the Fair…'

'Dark is Cynddylan's hall tonight,
With no fire, no songs.
My cheek is worn out with tears.'

'Silent is Cynddylan's hall tonight
After having lost its lord;
Great God of mercy, what shall I do?'

THE FALL OF THE PICTS

During the 8th century the intermarriage of Pictish and Scottish royalty began to produce leaders with claims to both kingdoms. Occasionally, Scots became kings of the Picts, although more often the Picts dominated the Scots. Yet there was also a strong sense of nationalism, and both populations fought for their independence.

The balance of power was upset by the arrival of the Vikings in the early 9th century. The Vikings conducted daring raids into the heart of Pictish territory, which the Scots saw as an opportunity to free Dalriada. In 834, as the Pictish king Oengus II faced a Viking raid in the north, the Dalriadan leader Alpin rebelled, forcing the Picts to split their army in two. On Easter Day the first Pictish army was defeated at the hands of the Scots, and Alpin marched north to attack the rear of the second Pictish army, who had successfully seen off the Vikings. In the second battle, however, the Scots were brutally defeated and Alpin slain by Oengus, who 'cut off his head'.

Alpin was succeeded by his son, Kenneth, who allied himself with the Vikings against the Picts. In 839 the Picts suffered a disastrous defeat at the hands of the Norsemen in which the High King Eogainn, his brother Bran, and 'numberless others' were killed. The slaughter of the Pictish nobility and warrior elite opened Kenneth MacAlpine's claim to the vacant Pictish throne and a chance to re-establish Causantin Mac Fergus' dynasty over both peoples.

The vagaries of matrilineal succession meant that several others had an equal claim, and Drust IX actually took the throne. What happened next is unclear, but it is believed that MacAlpine attacked and destroyed the remnants of the Pictish army in 841, and then, according to legend, he invited the surviving claimants to the throne from all seven Pictish Royal Houses to a feast to settle things peacefully.

They brought together as to a banquet all the nobles of the Picts, and taking advantage of their perhaps excessive potation and the gluttony of both drink and food, and noted their opportunity and drew out bolts which held up the boards; and the Picts fell into the hollows of the benches on which they were sitting, caught in a strange trap up to their knees, so that they could never get up; and the Scots immediately slaughtered them all... And thus the more warlike and powerful nation of the two peoples wholly disappeared; and the other, by far inferior in every way, as a reward obtained in the time of so great a treachery, have held to this day the whole land from sea to sea, and called it Scotland after their name.

While not exactly history, this story certainly explains how the Scots could inherit the land when 'the Picts were far superior in arms'. Kenneth moved his capital to Scone and brought the relics of St Columba, including the Stone of Destiny. A hostile take-over by Kenneth is supported by the fact that the Picts resisted Scottish domination. After the short reign of MacAlpine's

Situated in the town of Forres, the 6.5 metre-high (21 ft) Sueno's Stone could be considered a Pictish 'Trajan's Column'. On one side is an intricate Celtic cross, and on the other are carved over 100 warlike figures. The badly weathered top appears to show three long-robed figures with crossed hands – perhaps there were once five, but they may also be the Holy Trinity or a depiction of the triplicate war-goddess. Below them assemble the cavalry and what is obviously the king and four companions.

In the middle third of the stone is a great battle. Champions duel before a watching crowd and battle-horns trumpet. Swordsmen follow archers into battle, preceded by what might be an uncharacteristically cramped attempt at more cavalry, or alternatively war dogs and their handlers. In the centre, staff-carrying priests ring a Celtic church quadrangular bell, signalling victory, and the stack of seven decapitated bodies and heads suggest a ritual beheading of captive enemies, perhaps one trophy for each Pictish king. The lower third shows a second battle, and at the bottom the victors chasing off the losers. There are more beheadings held underneath an arch or bridge. One head in particular is displayed publicly in a cage underneath the structure.

The stone dates from the 9th century, and there have been many suggestions as to what event it depicts. The style of the images, utilising dozens of small figures, is common on Irish crosses, leading some to theorise that it was erected by Kenneth MacAlpine to celebrate his victory over the Picts. However, Sueno's Stone is a Pictish-style cross-slab, not an Irish free-standing cross, and the cross-side is carved with typically Pictish vine-scroll, indicating Pictish workmanship. Kenneth MacAlpine is also unlikely to have risked offending his Pictish subjects with such a provocative image of defeat and subjugation. The best clue to the subject is the fact that two separate battles are depicted, suggesting that it commemorates the double Pictish victory over the Norsemen and Alpin of Dalriada in AD 834, with the specially displayed head being that of Alpin himself.

second son, the capital was moved back to the Pictish seat at Fortevoit, and an attempt was made to revive Pictish matrilineal succession by bringing to the throne the son of Kenneth's daughter by the 'King of the Britons', who reigned for ten years. For several generations the custom of matrilinear descent continued, but only within the MacAlpine Dynasty, until in 858 Domnall I proclaimed that both Pict and Scot would live under one set of laws (a Dalriadan one), and the Scots and Picts were forever united.

In the end the Picts disappeared through a process of cultural colonialism. Gaelic replaced Pictish as the language of the nobility, Pictish fashions were replaced by Scottish ones, and Scottish myths and stories told by Scottish bards replaced Pictish tales. Early Scottish cross-slabs, though in the Pictish style and obviously created by Pictish carvers, show no Pictish symbols, suggesting that the outward marks of being a Pict, such as warrior tattoos, might mark one as an enemy of the king, and were quickly discontinued. The population began to be called Scots, as they lived in Scotland now, and their Pictish ancestry was gradually forgotten.

THE REMAINS OF THE PICTS

Hundreds of Pictish symbol-stones are found throughout Scotland, and there are many guide-books available. While many stones are free to be viewed by the public, others are on private land, or have been removed to museums. Some of the best are in:

Aberlemno Churchyard	McManus Galleries
Dunrobin Castle Museum	Meffan Museum
Elgin Museum	Meigle Museum and
Groam House Museum	Meigle Primary School
Inverness Museum	Tankerness Museum, Orkney
and Art Gallery	Perth Museum & Art Gallery
Marischal Museum	Woodhill House

The best collection of Pictish artefacts is held by the National Museum of Scotland in Chambers Street, Edinburgh, Scotland.

http://www.nms.ac.uk/
email: info@nms.ac.uk

The town of Burghhead, Moray, contains the ruins of a great Pictish fort, and also hosts the 'Burning of the Clavie', a Hogmanay festival of Pictish origin, which takes place on the original Hogmanay night of 11 January.

Orkney also has a rich collection of Pictish and other ancient sites, including the Pictish settlement at the Brough of Birsay, Buckquoy and the Broch of Guerness.

Kilmartin House in Argyll, traces the 5,000-year history of the Kilmartin Valley, including the Dark Age capital of the Scots, Dunnadd. The famous Pictish boar and ogham inscription carved by Pictish conquerors are weathering badly, and may soon be lost forever.

Kilmartin, Argyll, Scotland, PA31 8RQ.
E-mail: museum@khouse.demon.co.uk
http://www.kilmartin.org/

Musical instruments from the Pictish era, such as the carnyx and Pictish triple-pipes, can be heard on *The Kilmartin Sessions*, an excellent CD available from Kilmartin House. More carnyx recordings are available from:

Carnyx & Co
69 Spottiswoode Street
Edinburgh EH9 1DL
Scotland
http://www.carnyx.mcmail.com/
email: carnyx@mcmail.com

The Picts are not a popular subject for re-enactment, maybe because an accurate Pictish outfit does not meet the generally accepted minimum safety standards. However, there are many groups who recreate other Dark Age cultures, and one with an active Pictish contingent is:

Britannia
http://www.arthurian.freeuk.com/
email: britannia@arthurian.freeuk.com

Of wider interest is the Pictish Arts Society, a focus for study and discussion of all aspects of Pictish and early Scottish history. For further information contact :

Pictish Arts Society
27 George Square, Edinburgh
Scotland EH8 9LD
http://www.pictarts.demon.co.uk/index.htm
email: info@pictarts.demon.co.uk

In 1977 Brian Robertson ('Robbie the Pict') declared the Pictish Free State on Skye. The Pictish High Commission can be contacted by email to: robbiethepict@pictland.freeserve.co.uk

Every year on 20 May the members of the state celebrate Pictish independence on Dunnichen Day, holding a remembrance ceremony on Dunnichen Hill, near the town of Forfar, Angus.

The Eriskay Pony Society exists to promote and protect the ancient Pictish horse. For further details contact

Eriskay Pony Society
Hardiston House, Cleish, Kinross
Scotland KY137LP
Email: catrionam.cochrane@virgin.net

SELECTED BIBLIOGRAPHY

Printed primary sources

Adomnan, *Life of Columba.*

Aneurin *Y Gododdin.*

Bede, *Historia Ecclesiastica gentis Anglorum.*
   Venerabilis Bedae Opera Historica.
   Chronicum Scotum.

Dunn, Joseph (trans.) *Táin Bó Cúalnge,* 1914.

Gildas, *De Excidio Britanniae.*

Hen, Canu Llywarch, *Marwnad Cynddylan.*

Hull, Standish, O'Grady and Hayes (trans.) *The Cuchullin Saga,* 1898.

Koch, John T. (Ed.) *The Celtic Heroic Age: Literary Sources for Ancient Celtic Europe and Early Ireland and Wales,* 1995.

Ni Sh`eaghda, Nessa (Ed., trans.), *T`oruigheacht Dhiarmada agus Ghr`ainne,* 1967.

Skene, William, *Chronicle of the Picts and Scots and other early memorials of Scottish History,* 1876.

Skene, William F. (Ed.), *The Four Ancient Books of Wales: Containing the Cymric Poems attributed to the Bards of the Sixth Century,* 1964.

Tacitus, *Annals.*

William, John ab Ithel, *The Traditional Annals of the Cymry,* 1867.

Williams, Ifor *The poems of Llywarch Hen,* 1932.

Williams ab Ithel, Rev. John (Ed.), *Annales Cambriæ,* 1860.

Winterbottom, Michael (Ed), *The Ruin of Britain and Other Works,* 1978.

Secondary sources

Alcock, Leslie, *Economy, Society, and Warfare Among the Britons and Saxons 400-800 AD,* 1987.

Alcock, L., *The Neighbours of the Picts: Angles, Britons and Scots at War and at Home,* 1993

Anderson, Joseph and Douglas, David (Eds.), *Scotland in Pagan Times: The Iron Age,* 1883.

Anderson, M.O., *Kings and Kingship in Early Scotland,* 1973.

Bannerman, J., *Studies in the History of Dalriada,* 1974.

Beck, R.W., *Scotland's Native Horse,* 1992.

Brooke, Daphne, *Wild Men and Holy Places,* 1995.

Carver, Martin, *Surviving in Symbols, A Visit to the Pictish Nation,* 1999.

Chadwick, H.M., *Early Scotland,* 1949.

Crawford, B. Earl & Mormaer, *Norse-Pictish relationships in Northern Scotland,* 1995.

Cummings, W.A., *The Age of the Picts,* 1995.
   The Picts and their Symbols, 1999.

Ellis, Peter Berresford, *Celt vs Saxon.*

Epstein, Angelique Gulermovich, *War Goddess: The Morrigan and her Germano-Celtic Counterparts.*

Foster, Sally M., *Picts, Gaels and Scots,* 1996.

Gilbert, I., *The Symbolism of the Pictish Stones in Scotland,* 1995.

Henderson, Isabel, *The Picts,* 1967.

Henderson, Isabel, *The Art & Function of Rosemarkies Pictish Monuments,* 1989.

Jackson, Anthony, *The Pictish Trail*, 1989.
   The Symbol Stones of Scotland, 1989.
Jackson, Kenneth, *Language and history in early Britain*, 1953.
Laing, Ian and Jennifer, *The Picts and the Scots*, 1993.
Laing, Lloyd, *The Archaeology of Late Celtic Britain and Ireland
   400–1200AD*, 1975.
Lethbridge, T. C., *The Painted Men*, 1954.
McCone, Kim R., *Werewolves, Cylopes, Diberga and Fianna*, 1986.
Nagy, Joseph Falaky, *The Wisdom of the Outlaw*.
Nicoll, Eric (Ed.), *Pictish Panorama*, 1997.
Ritchie, Anna, *The Kingdom of the Picts*, 1977.
   The Picts, 1989.
   Perceptions of the Picts: from Eumenius to John Buchan, 1993.
   *Picts: An Introduction to the Life of the Picts and the Carved Stones
   in the Care of the Secretary of State for Scotland*, 1989.
Sayers, William, 'Martial Feats in the Old Irish Ulster Cycle',
   Canadian Journal of Irish Studies, Vol.9:1 (June 1983).
Scott, Archibald B., *The Pictish Nation: its People & its Church*, 1918.
Small, Alan (Ed.), *The Picts – A New Look at Old Problems*, 1987.
Smyth, Alfred, *Warlords and Holy Men*, 1984.
Stevenson, John, *Pictish Symbol Stones*, 1998.
Sutherland, E., *In Search of the Picts*, 1994.
   Pictish Guide, 1995.
Frederick Wainright, *The Problem of the Picts*, 1955.

GLOSSARY

Bard A sub-class of Druid, singers and poets also entrusted with education, and who survived the coming of Christianity.

Broch A distinctive type of circular stone fort.

Brythonic One branch of the Celtic family of languages, as distinct from Goidelic.

Caledonian The dominant tribe of the central Highlands in Roman times, later a general term for Britons living north of Antonine Wall.

Celt General term for the inhabitants of central and western Europe in the Iron Age, and their descendants up until the present, usually defined by language.

Clan Kinship group defined by descent from a common ancestor.

Cenedl Welsh for clan.

Ceathernach The medieval equivalent of the *fianna*, anglicised as 'kern' or 'cateran', a group of young warriors.

Cantref Welsh for *Ceathernach* (see above).

Cú Chulainn 'Hound of Chullain', a mythical Ulster hero.

Druids The intellectual, artistic and priestly class of Celtic society.

Cruithni Literally 'people of the designs', the Goidelic rendering of *Pritani* or 'Briton'.

Currach A hide boat.

Feat *Chleas* in Gaelic, a general term for martial abilities or tricks.

Fianna Irish term for a group of young warriors who live outside the tribal structure.

Goidelic One branch of the Celtic family of languages, as distinct from Brythonic.

La Tene Archaeological site in Austria dated to the late Iron Age, and Celtic school of art associated with that find.

Mabinogi, the Collection of Welsh tales and folklore.

Mac Gaelic prefix meaning 'son of', equivalent of *ap* in Welsh or *maqq* in Pictish.

Matrilinear succession Determination of royal lineage through the female blood-line.

Mormaer A noble rank in early medieval Scotland, roughly equivalent to an earl.

Morrigan, the The Irish war-goddess, the triplicate *Morrigan* ('Great Queen') / *Nemain* ('Battle Frenzy') / *Babd Catha* ('Battle Crow').

Ogham A writing system of Irish origin.

P-Celtic See Brythonic.

Q-Celtic See Goidelic.

Scotti Roman name for an Irish tribe or Irish generally.

Toiseach Pictish noble rank, roughly equivalent to an earl.

Woad A herb native to Britain that contains *indigin*, and was used for dying.

COLOUR PLATE COMMENTARY

PLATE A: CALEDONIAN TRIBESMAN, AD 200

The weapons wielded by the early Picts must have derived substantially from those of the Caledonian tribes. This warrior (1) is clad in long tartan trousers or trews, and his helmet (2) is of the contemporary British type, decorated with enamel in a similar 'Ultimate La Tene' style to his bodypaint. Tacitus noted that the Caledonians used small round bucklers (3), while Herodian said they used long oval shields (4). The main missile weapon was the spear (5), which had a hollow brass butt and was rattled to frighten enemies. He wears an armband (9), and a torc (10) around his neck.

His sword (6, and scabbard 6a) is a native British type, although Tacitus describes the Caledonian swords at Mons Grampius as not just 'long', but as *ingentes gladii* ('giant swords'). Such remarkable language was also used to describe the *hasta ingens* and *hasta enorma* ('enormous lance') in the German arsenal of the same era, referring to 2.5 metre-long (7 ft) fire-hardened oak halberds, some of which have been excavated in Lower Saxony. The illustrated weapon (7) is a hypothetical fire-hardened wooden sword that may have been the Caledonian equivalent.

Also depicted is a carnyx (8), an extraordinary Celtic trumpet shown on the Gundestrup Cauldron. This example, recovered from a bog near Deskford, Scotland, dates from between AD 100-300 and has a handsome wild boar's head, with eyes of red enamel and a movable wooden tongue. Diodorus Siculus reported 'their trumpets again are of a peculiar barbarian kind; they blow into them and produce a harsh sound which suits the tumult of war'; in fact, the 'barbarian' carnyx is one of the most sophisticated musical instruments ever made, as well as one of the loudest. A carnyx was capable of a startling range of tones, from a deep drone to a high, shrill trumpet, textured by a buzz, growl or rattling drone. Outdoors, the carnyx could be heard at a tremendous distance, as it was held vertically four feet over the heads of the battling warriors, and both the wooden tongue and the jaws moved as if alive.

PLATE B: SCATHA'S SCHOOL OF WAR

In this plate the legendary Scatha is shown teaching Cú Chulainn a special technique or 'feat' with sword and buckler. According to the Irish tales, Scatha's island was found either 'in the east of Alba' or on the Isle of Skye, where local tradition places it at Dunsgaith (*Dun Scatha*).

It is perhaps striking that specialised institutions existed for advanced martial training, and that these arts would be taught by women. The participation of women might be explained by the spiritual or magical aspect of their activities. In Ireland it was a druidess, Bodbmall, who trained Finn mac Cumaill; Buanann 'taught the use of arms to the fiana', and in Wales, Peredur was trained by nine 'witches' who fought in helmets and armour and had the Druidic gift of prophesy. In Pictland Scatha, the 'Shadowy One', was described as a prophetess and sage, and Cú Chulainn had to fight her rival Aife and several other 'hags'. When Fionn chased Oscar and Diarmuid to Pictland and was unable to overcome them, he also enlisted a 'hag' to 'practice magic against him'.

This supernatural side to female involvement suggests that the women warriors were not merely martial artists, but represented a Druidic class, perhaps priestesses teaching the secret arts of the war goddess to a few chosen heroes. The Celtic war-goddess, best known as the Irish triplicate *Morrigan*, appeared under many names but was always translated as *Victoria*, 'the victorious one', by the Romans, and was invoked by both the Gauls and Britons before battle.

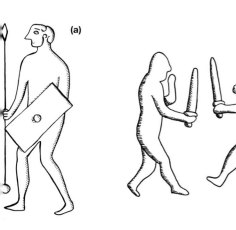

Did the Picts fight naked?
(a) The 'naked' spearman as depicted on Collessie, Balgavies and Rhynie. His large rectangular shield is that of the ancient Caledonians shown on the nearby Antonine Wall, and probably does not depict a contemporary Pict, but rather an ancient hero.
(b) Two 'naked' Picts from Shandwick, Easter Ross. This is a hunting scene, not a battle, and these figures may either be engaged in a formal duel, or perhaps a sword-dance, in either case suggesting a ritual element to such combat.
(c) Two Picts from St Andrews duel 'naked', while a female figure, also seemingly naked, dances between them, above two ravens.
(d) Spearman with only a cloak, from Eassie, Angus.

'Boudica then raised her hands to heaven and said 'I thank you, Andrasta, and call upon you as woman speaking to woman...I beg you for victory and preservation of liberty...Mistress, be forever our leader'.

The Morrigan was closely associated with ravens, for obvious reasons; clouds of carrion birds would follow Celtic armies, eager to feed off the inevitable dead. Like the Norse Valkyries, who carried the dead from the field of battle to paradise in Valhalla, the Celtic Morrigan also performed a function as a 'psychopomp', devouring the bodies of the fallen heroes in the form of a carrion bird and transporting them to the otherworld. The Celtiberians saw the Morrigan in the form of their local carrion bird, as Silius Italicus noted: '...for they believe that the soul goes up to the gods in heaven, if the body is devoured on the field by the hungry vulture'.

The Morrigan survived as an important being even after the coming of Christianity, and in the 9th-century Irish tales, *morrigna* were harpy-like monsters in female form, 'hooded crows, or women of the sid...not demons of hell but demons of the air' who dwelt 'in rough places yonder...where the raven-women instigate battle' and then claimed their due after the slaughter. Even in 18th-century Scotland, the *Cailleach* or *Skadi* was feared in the Highlands in the form of raven and hooded crow.

There may also be a connection with the strange bird-masked figures on Pictish stones. A clue to their nature can be found when Cú Chulainn fights the 'one-eyed hag' in Pictland, who is named 'Eis Enchenn, the bird-headed', mother of three of Aife's champions. 'Enchenn' here is an *enchendach*, a bird-feather mask or cloak worn in totemistic ceremonies, and mentioned as being worn by druids such as Cathbad. This would suggest that the Pictish figures are raven-masked priests or priestesses, whose appeasement of the war goddess may have been considered too important to be extirpated by the Pictish church. Similarly, the carved deer heads may also have been ritual masks, and dog or wolf-masked figures are also recorded on Pictish stones. Such costumes may have been more than ceremonial; the *Black*

Book of Carmarthen contains a reference to Arthur fighting dog-heads at Dun-Eidyn (Edinburgh):

Though Arthur was but playing,
blood was flowing
in the hall of Afarnach
fighting with a hag.
He pierced the cudgel-head
in the halls of Dissethach
On the mount of Eidyn
they fought Dog-heads;
by the hundred they fell.

PLATE C: PICTISH BOATS

Both the Picts and the Scots were known to the Roman primarily as sea raiders, and sea power was a vital part c their military strength. Celtic boats were *currachs*, mad from hide stretched over a frame. Caesar implies frames c wickerwork, while the monks of Iona ordered wood for ' 'long ship', probably for the frame and mast.

At up to 50 feet long, *currachs* were not small. Allectus coins show them as high-riding vessels with up to seve oars each side and a single sail, while the Irish Broighte model boat has nine rowing benches and oar holes throug the hull, a steering oar set on the port side, and a mast an yard. The St Orland's Stone shows a Pictish boat wit several oars, and the Dalriadan *Senchus Fer n Alba* specifies seven-bench boats. Medieval Highland galley were crewed by two or three men per oar in wartime, an

Strange bird-headed figures often adorn Pictish stones.
(a) from Murthly in Perthshire, this may be a representation of 'Eis Enchenn, the bird-headed' fighting the Hound of Ulster, or represent the rival warrior cults of the raven-goddess and the 'dog-heads'.
(b) from Rossie Priory.
(c) from Hunter's Hill, with a smaller animal-headed attendant.
(d) two raven-masked figures holding a severed head between their beaks, from Papil, Shetland.

The Pictish boat from the Cossans cross-slab. Weathering has obscured the figure in the prow, and it is often mistaken for a 'large object'.

Adomnan's descriptions confirm that the Scottish ships could carry over 20 people, indicating at least two men per oar. With navies as large as the 140 boats maintained by Dalriada, and the 150 Pictish ships wrecked off Ross in 736, the northern Celts could swiftly transport thousands of warriors huge distances by sea, and fight major campaigns from Orkney to Man. At least one great sea battle is recorded between *Cenel nGarbar* and *Cenel nLoairn* in 719.

These ships were capable of long voyages, and Tim Severin's recreation voyage in the *Brendan* proved that *currachs* could sail intact as far as America. In the 4th century Theodosius pursued a Pictish fleet to 'Thule', which was the name Ptolmy, Pytheas and the Irish monks gave to Iceland. Hordes of Roman coins from the period AD 270-305 have been found in Iceland, presumably placed there by retreating Pictish pirates. This plate shows a Pictish *currach* approaching the coast of Iceland in order to recover their looted Roman silver.

PLATE D: PICTISH RAID ON HADRIAN'S WALL, AD 360

The early Pictish elite supported itself by raiding Roman Britain from land and sea. To them, Britain was a rich, under-defended land, and silver hordes such as the Mildenhall Treasure and the Traprain Law Horde were clearly buried to hide riches from Pictish raiders.

From the first mention of the Picts, raiding was their primary occupation, which the Romans seemed powerless to stop. In AD 343 the emperor came to Britain and entered in to truce with them, but by 360 'savage tribes of *Scotti* and *Picti*, having broken the truce, were ravaging the part of Roman Britain in the neighbourhood of the wall', and over the next seven years 'the *Picti*, *Saxones*, *Scotti* and *Atecotti* harassed the Britons continually'.

The raids of the 360s were not the random rages of uncivilised barbarians, but appear to have been carefully planned and coordinated by an unusually capable man, almost certainly the Pictish High King. He had no thought of conquest, only of the riches that Roman Britain could provide, and his masterplan, the *Conspiratio Barbarica*, was a stroke of criminal genius.

The Picts coordinated with tribes in Ireland, the Hebrides, and as far away as Gaul and Germany. Ships were built, war bands trained and assembled. Front-line militia units and agents of the *Arcani* (a kind of Roman secret service) were bribed to keep silent. Then, on the appointed day in 368, a single massive attack was launched on the Roman Empire. The Picts, Scots and Saxons launched hundreds of multiple sea-borne raids, and more Picts poured over the wall. The *Alemanni* broke into Gaul and other tribes attacked central Europe. Fullufaudes, 'Duke of the Britons', was ambushed with his army as he rushed from York. Nectarides, 'Count of the Saxon Shore', and his fleet were destroyed at sea by the Saxons. The badly mauled army retreated in confusion and sat immobilised in their barracks, giving the Picts free reign throughout the country.

Although it was the most devastating raid ever reported from Britain, it was not a conquest, and the death toll was probably fairly low. The attacks on the Continent had little hope of equal success, but they did prevent fresh Roman forces from being immediately dispatched to Britain. By the time Theodosius arrived with reinforcements, the province had been picked clean, and many of the warrior bands had returned northwards.

Theodosius pursued the remaining raiding parties but a whole year passed before peace was restored. The Roman fleet conducted reprisal attacks on the Orkneys and Shetlands, and once more the Romans attempted to create a new province between the Walls. However, the slaves were gone and could not be replaced, and the Britons' confidence in Rome had been shattered. Most significantly, a whole tribe of captured *Alemanni* were shipped over as *foederati*, marking the start of Anglo-Saxon settlement in Britain.

During the period of Roman collapse the Picts expanded southwards under Drust Mac Erp, who 'reigned for 100 years and fought 100 battles'. Gildas said 'they seized the whole of the extreme north of the island from its inhabitants, right up to the wall', and raided deep into southern Britain, resulting in the need for Vortigern to invite Saxon warriors 'into the island like wolves into the fold, to beat back the peoples of the north'. Initially Hengist's cousins Octa and Ebissa attacked Orkney and established themselves 'as far as the borders of the Picts', but the Picts soon formed an alliance in support of the Saxon rebellion. Drust Mac Erp seems to have finally met his match in the legendary Arthur, who is believed to have fought several battles with the Picts, and expelled them from the Lowlands. This plate shows a Pictish raiding party surprising Romano-British defenders on Hadrian's Wall, as described by Gildas: 'there was no respite from the barbed grappling irons flung by their naked opponents, which tore our wretched countrymen from the walls and dashed them to the ground'.

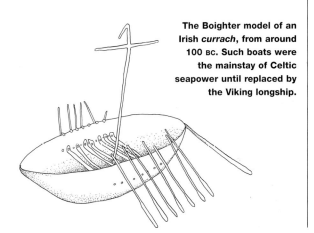

The Boighter model of an Irish *currach*, from around 100 BC. Such boats were the mainstay of Celtic seapower until replaced by the Viking longship.

PLATE E: PICTISH WEAPONRY

The remains of Pictish armour and weapons are few and fragmentary, and reconstructions must be made by matching the iconographic evidence with contemporary finds from elsewhere in Britain, Ireland and Europe.

The helmet types (1) and (2) are typical Dark Age helmets, based on late Roman models, and most likely looted from Roman, British or Saxon foes. The swords are of various styles; (3) is similar to contemporary Irish swords, with bone and antler fittings, (4) is based on a possible 10th-century Pictish sword in the National Museum of Scotland, and is what most Pictish carvings appear to depict, while (5) shows an Anglian influence, topped by a pommel from Moray. The scabbard (6) is tipped by a decorated chape from the St Ninian's Horde. (7) is a reconstruction of the late-Roman model crossbow, a weapon that uniquely survived in Pictish use throughout the Dark Ages, primarily as a hunting weapon.

The shields are of the basic types shown on carved stone; (8) is square, (9) is the H-shape held by 'David' on the St Andrew's sarcophagus, and (10) is round. All of these would be held with a simple punch-grip.

Axes and spears came in a wide variety of head shapes. Shown here are (11) a simple wedge, (12) a distinctive Pictish square head, (13) a two-handed battle-axe and (14) a stout spear with a broad blade, as described in *The Destruction of Da Dergas Hostel*.

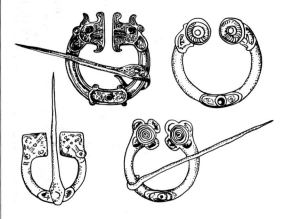

Four examples of Pictish penannular brooches.

PLATE F: PICTISH WARRIORS, AD 690

During the mid-7th century Northumbria expanded aggressively into southern Scotland, and Bede claimed that the Northumbrian king 'subjected most of the Picts to English rule'. The Picts were certainly not conquered or occupied, but it seems Iona pressured them to accept Northumbrian overlordship, since both Oswald and Oswiu (sons of King Aethelfrith of Bernicia) grew up in exile in Iona and supported the Columban church in Northumbria.

In 664 the southward-expanding Celtic church met the Romans coming north, and held the famous Synod of Whitby. When Northumbria switched allegiance to Rome, Iona withdrew its recognition of Northumbrian suzerainty. Oswiu's successor, Ecgfrith, attempted to regain this militarily, and in 672 he massacred a Pictish army at Carron.

A medieval Hebridean grave slab showing the quilted leather aketon or *cotun*, perhaps worn by the Golspie Pict and the 'king' on Sueno's Stone. Usually believed to have arrived in Europe with the Crusaders, the Aztecs also invented similar armour, so an independent development by the Picts cannot be ruled out.

Afterwards the Picts were again 'reduced to slavery and remained subject under the yoke of captivity', indicating that Ecgfrith extracted heavy tribute from them.

In response, the Picts elected a new king, Bruide Mac Bili, brother to Owen the Bald of Strathclyde. Bruide united and invigorated his demoralised people, retaking Dunnottar and Orkney and conquering Dunnadd. Then, on 20 May 685, he led an army of Picts, Scots and Britons to the most important Celtic victory since Mount Badon.

Dunnichen Moss or Nechtansmere was probably fought near the town of Forfar, Angus. The Northumbrians were lured in between the hill-fort of Dun Nechtan and a boggy loch called Nechtan's Mere or, in the Irish annals, *Linn Garan* ('the Pool of Herons'). Bede described how Ecgfrith 'rashly led an army to ravage the province of the Picts. The enemy pretended to retreat, and lured the king into narrow mountain passes, where he was killed with the greater part of his forces.'

In one mighty victory, the Picts recovered all the territory lost and pushed the Angles back beyond the Lammermuir Hills. In 698 there was another invasion, but Bruide once again destroyed the Northumbrian host.

This plate shows the sort of warriors that would have won this great Pictish victory. The infantryman's equipment is minimal – he is barefoot, dressed in a knee-length tunic, armed with a two-handed spear, javelins, a sword and a buckler. The cavalryman wears the sort of full equipment that would have been restricted to the Pictish kings, with a helmet and scale armour, and armed with a sword, a shield slung over his back, and lance. The detail of scale construction is based on the example found in Perthshire.

PLATE G: THE LAW OF THE INNOCENTS

Here we see Adomnan, Abbot of Iona, and his mother viewing the aftermath of a battle between Picts and Northumbrians, and coming across a slain warrior woman with an infant still clinging at her breast. This scene so distressed the Abbot's mother that she forced him to propose the 'Law of the Innocents', forbidding women to fight or command warriors, and which was ratified at the Synod of Birr in Ireland in 697 by 51 Celtic kings and 40 churchmen.

The presence of Pictish women on the battlefield is a good example of where popular perception and academic scepticism clash. Certainly, there were female combatants in other Celtic societies – although only 10 per cent of continental Celtic female graves contain weapons, and over half these are ornamental, this still leaves a significant number of women's graves with battle-scarred weapons, heroes' torcs and chariots. In early Ireland, several women were members of the *fianna*, while the use of arms was a legal requirement of landed women. Warrior queens like Macha of the Red Hair, Maeve of Connaught, Creidne the Feinid, and the British queens Cartimandua and Boudicca won their fame on the battlefield. Petronius describes a female British gladiator who fought from a chariot, and medieval Scottish and Irish women were also frequently involved in warfare, particularly as commanders.

While women are rarely depicted on Pictish stones, it is reasonable to assume that the Picts were similiar to other Celtic peoples in this respect. The common references in Irish tales to female fighters in Alba suggest that, if anything, women warriors were more common among the Picts. It can be further argued that Adomnan is unlikely to have convinced nearly 100 Celtic leaders to specifically exempt women from the legal responsibility of being warriors or military commanders unless there were a real need, and Pictish women were fighting and dying in battle. It is plausible to conclude that, prior to 700, the Picts allowed and/or required women to fight.

PLATE H: BATTLE WITH STRATHCLYDE, 744

The candidates for the Pictish throne were expected to be experienced warriors, and the Picts valued valour and martial prowess in their leaders as much as any other Celtic people. Sometimes they gained the throne itself by force of arms – one of the disadvantages of the Pictish matrilinear tradition was that there were always large numbers of eligible would-be kings, and when the democratic system failed, the results could be ugly. Between 726 and 729 four candidates for the throne fought at least nine pitched battles, before the mighty Oengus Mac Fergus emerged the victor.

The advantage of such bloody political selection was that the successful contender would inevitably be a strong and resourceful leader, and Oengus proved to be a great warrior king. In 734 he captured and drowned the king of the Northern Picts, in 736 he beheaded the Scottish king and became the first king of both Picts and Scots; and in 740 he crushed a Northumbrian invasion.

The dominant power in the north was the British kingdom of Strathclyde, which ruled lowland Scotland from Clyde to Solway from their great fortress capital at Dumbarton. The Strathclyde Britons had an enviable military history, and Oengus must have seen them as a challenge. In 744 he attacked and defeated them, a truly remarkable achievement that is almost certainly the great battle celebrated on the Aberlemno Battle Stone, which probably dates from the mid-8th century. This plate shows the battle as depicted at Aberlemno, with a central Pictish *schiltron* repelling the Strathclyde cavalry, while flanking Pictish horsemen sweep around to envelop them.

An ancient Briton from John *Speed's Historie of Great Britaine* (1611).

covered wagon from a lost stone from Meigle, Perthshire.

INDEX

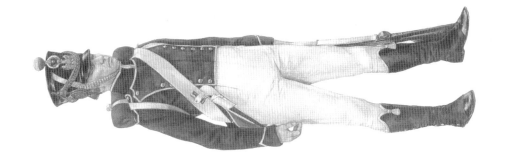

OSPREY
PUBLISHING

FIND OUT MORE ABOUT OSPREY

❏ Please send me the latest listing of Osprey's publications

❏ I would like to subscribe to Osprey's e-mail newsletter

Title / rank

Name

Address

City / county

Postcode / zip   state / country

e-mail

WAR

I am interested in:

❏ Ancient world
❏ Medieval world
❏ 16th century
❏ 17th century
❏ 18th century
❏ Napoleonic
❏ 19th century

❏ American Civil War
❏ World War 1
❏ World War 2
❏ Modern warfare
❏ Military aviation
❏ Naval warfare

Please send to:

North America:
Osprey Direct , 2427 Bond Street, University Park, IL 60466, USA

UK, Europe and rest of world:
Osprey Direct UK, P.O. Box 140, Wellingborough, Northants, NN8 2FA, United Kingdom

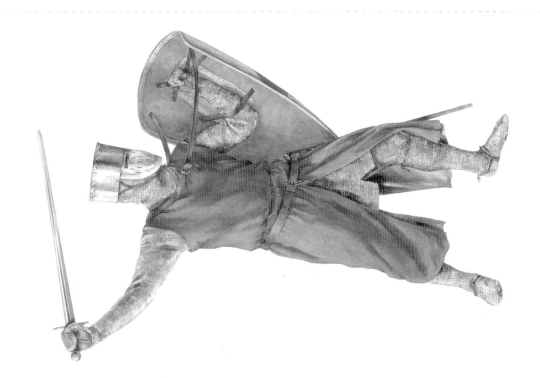

OSPREY
PUBLISHING

www.ospreypublishing.com

call our telephone hotline
for a free information pack

USA & Canada: 1-800-826-6600
UK, Europe and rest of world call:
+44 (0) 1933 443 863

Young Guardsman
Figure taken from *Warrior 22: Imperial Guardsman 1799–1815*
Published by Osprey
Illustrated by Richard Hook

Knight, c.1190
Figure taken from *Warrior 1: Norman Knight 950 – 1204 AD*
Published by Osprey
Illustrated by Christa Hook

POSTCARD

www.ospreypublishing.com